D1124595

SOUTH AFRICA

SOUTH AFRICA TROUBLED LAND

by *Elaine Pascoe*

Franklin Watts
New York/London/Toronto/Sydney/1987

27961

Photographs courtesy of: Photo Researchers, Inc.: p. 11
(top—Ray Ellis); Impact Visuals: pp. 11 (bottom—Catherine
D. Smith), 14 (both—Tony Savino); SATOUR: p. 21; New York
Public Library Picture Collection: pp. 29, 35, 42, 57;
The Bettmann Archive, Inc.: pp. 53, 55, 79; UPI/Bettmann
Newsphotos: pp. 66, 94, 114; UPI/Bettmann Newsphotos/Reuters:
pp. 76, 90, 99, 108, 110; AP/Wide World Photos: p. 85.

Map courtesy of Vantage Art

Library of Congress Cataloging-in-Publication Data

Pascoe, Elaine.
South Africa, troubled land.

Bibliography: p.
Includes index.
Summary: Examines the history and culture of
South Africa from its earliest European settlers
through the development of its diamond and mineral
resources and the establishment of apartheid to
the present.
1. South Africa—History—Juvenile literature.
[1. South Africa—History]   I. Title.
DT766.P29   1987   968   87-10735
ISBN 0-531-10432-X

CONTENTS

To my parents

1

CONTRASTS: BLACK AND WHITE

Albert Thipe works in Johannesburg, South Africa's largest city. He doesn't live there, however, because he is black—and Johannesburg's residential areas, by law, are reserved for whites. Instead, Albert lives in a men's hostel in Soweto, the sprawling, crowded black township outside Johannesburg. There he shares a dormitory room with a dozen other black men. Each morning he rises early, heats some water for shaving on a kerosene stove, and leaves to begin the hour-long bus ride to his factory job. He returns late in the day to cook a simple dinner on the same stove. Like the other men in the hostel, he has few possessions, and his rented furniture consists of a locker for his clothes and a simple bed.

Albert has a family, but his wife and their three children live hundreds of miles away in KwaZulu, an area set aside specifically for blacks. Until recently, laws prevented them from joining him in Soweto. Now the laws have been changed, but his family still cannot come: Women and children are not allowed in the hostels, and the other types of housing they might afford in Soweto are completely filled. Some families have moved to squatter camps, where they put up tin shacks in defiance of government regulations. But in these places, conditions are even more crowded and harsh than in the black townships. And there is always the chance that the police will come and tear the shacks down, making the residents homeless.

Nor can Albert live with his family in their village. Theirs is a farming community, but there is not enough land—and the land is too poor—for the family to make a living on it. Life there is hard. Albert's wife farms a small plot, but there is no opportunity for other work. The children go to school, but the oldest girl, who is thirteen, plans to leave next year to look for a job as a servant in a white household. Albert would like his children to continue their education, but he knows the chances are slim: Less than one percent of blacks in South Africa go on to universities.

So Albert continues to live apart from his family, visiting about once a year. On weekends, he sometimes goes to a soccer match or to the movies, but more often not. There are few bioscopes, or theaters, in Soweto, and he earns just enough to cover his basic living expenses, with a little left over to send to his family. In any case, the Soweto streets are dangerous at night. Gangs roam freely, and killings and beatings are common.

Herman Steyn has a farm near Cape Town, a stretch of rolling, green land ringed with distant mountains. Its vine-

Above: *a street in Soweto, the large township near Johannesburg, where many black workers live.* Below: *far from Johannesburg and far from Soweto, villagers in a black homeland gather at the well which supplies their water.*

yards, fields, and orchards produce wine and fruit and other crops. The Steyn family has farmed this land for generations—they are Afrikaners, descendants of Dutch settlers who arrived in South Africa in the 1700s. The main farmhouse is in the traditional style, an H-shaped, gabled manor house built of brick and covered with stucco. Nearby is a second house, where Herman hopes one of his sons will one day live and help him run the farm. Green lawns and colorful gardens surround the homes. From the front lawn, Herman can just see the rooftops of the closest village, where neat white houses and a steepled church cluster around a central green.

The Steyn children are now away from home: one son at the university, studying engineering, and a second son and a daughter at a boarding school for well-to-do white children in Cape Town. While his wife runs the house or takes the family car on shopping trips to the village or to Cape Town, Herman oversees the work of the farm. Most of the hard labor is done by mixed-race, or coloured, workers and their families; there are also a few black workers who have contracted their labor for a year. The coloured families live in two- and three-room dirt-floored houses provided by the farm.

Where the workers are concerned, Herman has seen some changes in recent times. The men now earn the equivalent of ten to fifteen dollars a week—twice what they made in the 1970s—and are provided with uniforms and wood for cooking fires; women earn about half that. Two years ago, Herman had electricity put into their houses. And because of a growing concern over alcoholism, the workers no longer receive the daily bottle of wine, or *dop*, that was formerly part of their payment. Even with improvements in working conditions, it is increasingly hard to find workers who will stay on the farm—they know that they can earn more money in the factories of the cities.

Even so, life at the farm is good for the Steyns. There are servants to help in the house and to serve the ample meals in the dining room. The wine cellar is lined with full casks. And the farm's products find an eager market in the cities.

These two fictional portraits present some of the sharp contrasts that mark modern South Africa, a land where a person's future can be decided by the shade of his or her skin. The portraits are only examples—there are many black families in South Africa who are not separated like the Thipes, many coloureds who are considerably better off than the farm workers, and many whites who do not share the affluent life-style of the Steyns. But overall, wealth and poverty, privilege and want divide sharply along color lines.

South Africa is among the most wealthy African countries, awash in gold and other natural resources. But the wealth—and political power—are controlled by the country's approximately 4.5 million whites. Some 3.5 million people of mixed race and Asian descent have a limited voice in government, a voice only recently attained. The vast majority of the country's people—about 20 million blacks—are shut out of government and, for the most part, from opportunities for a better life.

The white government of South Africa has maintained this state of affairs through *apartheid,* a policy of strict racial segregation encoded into law. Under this policy, the country's tapestry of racial and ethnic groups are lumped into four racial categories: white, coloured, Asian, and black. Each group is to live separately and be educated separately; each has certain economic privileges. The goal is not to make the groups "separate but equal" (the doctrine used to justify segregation of blacks in the U.S. South before 1954) but to keep them separate and unequal— coloureds above blacks, and whites above all. In short, the goal is white supremacy.

Most of the laws that established formal apartheid were passed in this century, many in the late 1940s and 1950s.

But the concepts behind them, and many of the practices they seek to support, are much older—as old as the history of white settlement in South Africa. Racial discrimination has been part of the country's fabric for three hundred years. To many (but by no means all) whites, it is a morally correct and justifiable view. To blacks, it is an inescapable fact of daily life, a barrier that will always stand in their way.

Today, however, South Africa is a country in a state of flux, under pressure from within and without to change its racial policies. Abroad, the government faces international criticism and economic sanctions—trade barriers imposed by other countries that disapprove of apartheid. At home, it faces demonstrations, riots, and increasing amounts of bloodshed, as frustrated blacks take to the streets in an effort to break down the barriers that keep them second-class citizens in their own land. In the face of the pressure, some of the laws that kept apartheid in place have crumbled; others are weakening. The government itself no longer likes to use the term apartheid, a word that has become hateful to people everywhere.

Meanwhile, whites and blacks alike are torn by divisions over what path the country should take. In talking about South Africa, it's easy to slip into stereotypes— standardized pictures of what members of each group are like. In fact, the country's racial divisions are arbitrary, based on appearance and how a person is "generally accepted." Each group includes people with different backgrounds and cultures. Whites may be descended from

Above: *the modern home of a white beef farmer in Cape Province.* Below: *the kitchen of the farmhouse, though simple, is fully equipped with modern conveniences.*

English, Dutch, French, or other European settlers and speak English or Afrikaans (an offshoot of Dutch), both of which are official languages of the country. Coloureds may count Asians, whites, and blacks among their ancestors. Blacks may belong to any of several tribal groups and speak different tribal languages, as well as English or Afrikaans.

Just as backgrounds differ, so do politics. While coloured and various black groups in general share a desire for greater political and economic rights, they are by no means agreed on how to achieve those rights or even what form they should take. Whites are not all racists, and not all support apartheid. It was an Afrikaner, the Right Reverend Joost de Blank of Cape Town, who called apartheid "anti-Christian, inhuman, and . . . suicidal."

But most whites are not eager to give up their privileges, and many fear for their future under a majority government. Thus, for every step it takes to ease one aspect of the apartheid laws, the government seems to take another step to silence dissent and maintain its control of the situation. Backed by strong security forces, it is in a good position to do so. An end to white supremacy doesn't seem imminent in South Africa. And as long as white supremacy continues, it's likely that unrest, fighting, and the risk of a full-scale revolution will continue as well—and in all probability, increase.

South Africa's problems are a matter of concern for people everywhere, for several reasons. First is a practical matter: South Africa has strategic importance to the industrial world, especially to the Western democracies. It is a primary source of valuable minerals, not just gold but diamonds and many other vital substances used in industry and for military purposes. It is also a shipping point for minerals and resources from the rest of Africa. And, according to some estimates, half the world's shipping passes around the Cape of Good Hope, at the tip of South Africa. These ships include oil tankers carrying their precious cargo from the Persian Gulf to Europe; many are too large to take the alternate route through the Suez Canal. Also, the Soviet Union's interest in southern Africa has increased in recent times, and two of South Africa's neighbors, Angola and Mozambique, are oriented toward that country. For these reasons, then, stability and peace in South Africa are important to the West.

Beyond the practical reason for world concern is a moral question: Whether it is right for a small group to dominate the majority of a country's people on the basis of their race—or whether, indeed, race is a good reason for any type of discrimination. This question strikes a chord with many people in the United States, where blacks (as a minority group) have gained ground only slowly against racial prejudice. It has brought many Americans to support South African blacks in their struggle against apartheid.

In the United States, ending legal discrimination did not eliminate racial prejudice. In the same way, altering the laws in South Africa is not likely to end forms of discrimination that are deeply ingrained in the people. To find a solution, it is necessary to look into the country's past, at the forces that shaped the current situation.

2

SETTING
THE STAGE

In many ways, South Africa is a fortunate country. It is unusually, and at times breathtakingly, beautiful; dramatic mountains, rolling grasslands, gentle seacoasts, and harsh semideserts contribute to its vivid contrasts. Before modern times, it teemed with game, and game is still plentiful in many regions. More important to modern South Africa, however, has been what lies beneath the land: a richness of mineral resources.

Yet South Africa's good fortune has also helped create its major problem. The land has been the stage on which the drama of conflicts between black and white has been acted out, and it has also been the subject of conflict. The racial problems that tear the country apart today began in earlier times as disputes between black and white over control of the land itself.

THE LAND

Altogether, South Africa is about one-sixth the size of the United States. Ringed by the sea on three sides (the Atlantic Ocean to the west, and to the east the Indian Ocean), the land rises up from the coast in a series of plateaus divided by sharp cliffs and mountains. The mountains that rim these plateaus also separate them from the narrow coastal regions. In a satellite view, the country might look something like a large saucer, tipped slightly from north (where the land is highest) to south.

In the west and south, the mountains run almost to the sea. Beyond them are two dry tablelands, the Little Karroo (southernmost, inland from the tip of the Cape of Good Hope) and the Great Karroo. This area has traditionally been South Africa's garden—a farming and ranching region where much wine and fruit are produced and cattle and sheep are raised. The mountains of the west block rainfall, however, with the result that some farmland must be irrigated, and parts of the region are desert or semi-desert areas too dry for farming.

The most dramatic of South Africa's mountain ranges is the high, jagged Drakensberg Range, which runs from the south to the northeast parallel to the east coast, inland from a broad coastal plain. The South African writer Alan Paton described this region in the famous opening of his novel *Cry, the Beloved Country*:

> There is a lovely road that runs from Ixopo into the hills. These hills are grass-covered and rolling, and they are lovely beyond any singing of it. The road climbs seven miles into them, to Carisbrooke; and from there, if there is no mist, you look down on one of the fairest valleys of Africa. About you there is grass and bracken and you may hear the forlorn crying of the titihoya, one of the birds of the veld. Below you is the valley of the Umzimkulu, on its journey from the Drakensberg to the sea; and beyond and behind the river, great hill after great hill. . . .

Inland from the Drakensberg Range lies the Highveld, a high, rolling plateau covered with thickly matted grass and scattered bushes and trees. In places, flat-topped moun-

The Drakensberg Range in Natal
Province is one of the
most beautiful regions of South Africa.

tains jut abruptly out of the plain. The high plateaus roll on into the northeast corner of the country, the region known as the Transvaal. This is a farming area and also the site of South Africa's largest and most famous park—Kruger National Park—where zebras, elephants, leopards, lions, antelope, and other wild animals roam free.

The Transvaal also includes the Witwatersrand, an area that has been critical to South Africa in modern times. This region is the site of much of the country's mining and also a major manufacturing center. Few countries have mineral wealth to equal South Africa's: rich deposits of gold, diamonds, platinum (most of the world's supply), uranium, chrome, copper, manganese, nickel, silver, and tin; vast reserves of iron; and thick seams of coal. The only major resource lacking is petroleum.

The climate is variable but mild—even in the coldest months, freezing temperatures are rare along the coasts and only occasional inland. Nor are the warm months, except along the southeastern coast, too hot for comfort. Warm ocean currents give the southeastern coast a gentler, almost subtropical climate, making the broad and pleasant beaches there popular with vacationers. But overall the average mean temperature is about 60 degrees Fahrenheit (16° C).

In land and climate, then, nature dealt South Africa a good hand. But a few key cards are missing: The country has little in the way of forests, and none of its rivers is navigable. These deficiencies, combined with low rainfall and poor soil in many regions, kept the country from developing with the speed of other areas, such as North America. The largest river is the Orange, which rises in the Drakensberg Range and flows westward across the country to the Atlantic Ocean. The Vaal River, which originates in the Witwatersrand, feeds into it. A series of smaller rivers—the Fish, Sundays, Kei, and others—run from the Drakensberg Range to the Indian Ocean. The Limpopo, also flowing into the Indian Ocean, forms part of the country's northern border.

Modern South Africa is divided into four provinces: the Cape Province, which includes most of the west as well as the tip of the Cape of Good Hope; Natal, along the east coast; the Orange Free State, inland from Natal; and the Transvaal, in the northeast. There are three capital cities, one for each branch of the central government: Pretoria (the administrative capital) in the Transvaal; Cape Town (the legislative capital) in the Cape Province, at the southwestern tip of the country; and Bloemfontein (the judicial capital) in the Orange Free State. Johannesburg, in the heart of the Witwatersrand, is the largest city. Except for Cape Town, the mountainous and arid west coast has no major ports. On the milder east coast, important ports are Durban, East London, and Port Elizabeth.

South Africa's neighbors to the north are, from east to west, Mozambique, Swaziland, Zimbabwe, Botswana, and Namibia (South-West Africa). These countries are all former European colonies and, with the exception of Namibia, are now under some form of black majority rule. Namibia is a disputed territory administered by South Africa, and its future is a source of contention between South Africa and the rest of the international community. South Africa has another neighbor, too. Plunked into the middle of the country, and surrounded by South Africa on all sides, is the small nation of Lesotho.

But 350 years ago, none of these political boundaries existed. There were no cities, and South Africa's mineral wealth was a secret locked inside its mountains and beneath its plains. There was only the land, and the herds of game that roamed across it. And, of course, there were people.

SOUTH AFRICA'S EARLIEST PEOPLE

Europeans settled in what is now South Africa in the 1600s, but the area was populated long before that time.

Human ancestors lived there as long as two million years ago. At least two thousand years ago, nomadic hunters and gatherers lived in the area, going where game was plentiful. For the most part, their history—and that of their descendants for centuries—is lost in time.

In the 1500s, two groups descended from these early hunters and gatherers still lived in western and southern South Africa. They were the San and the Khoikhoi, both yellowish-skinned people who used stone tools. The San, whom the Europeans later called Bushmen, still followed the ways of their ancestors, moving from place to place in small groups to follow the game. They stood about 5 feet (1.5 m) tall, on the average, and hunted with poison-tipped arrows. The Khoikhoi (later called Hottentots by the Europeans) had developed a somewhat different way of life. In addition to hunting, they kept herds of cattle, sheep, and goats, and they moved with their herds in search of pastures. (Some anthropologists believe that the San also had begun to keep cattle, but the evidence is unclear.)

By this time, a third group of people had also entered the region. They were brown-skinned people who spoke various Bantu languages, and they moved down the continent from central Africa, perhaps as a result of wars and upheavals there. The migration took centuries, and, again, much of its history is lost. But archaeological evidence shows that the Bantu-speaking people were in South Africa as early as A.D. 900.

The Bantu-speakers comprised some two hundred tribal groups with different (but related) languages and cultures. They were organized into larger groups than the San or Khoikhoi, although the groups varied in size from less than one thousand to perhaps thirty-five thousand. They were more advanced than either the San or the Khoikhoi, too—they had iron tools and weapons, and, besides hunting and herding, they raised grain and other crops.

A Bantu village was a far more permanent settlement

than a San or Khoikhoi camp, typically consisting of round, thatch-roofed houses. But the settlements varied considerably, depending on the group. Some were small and widely scattered; others, especially in the north, were complex towns ringed by fields and grazing grounds. In many settlements, the houses were grouped into clusters, or kraals, belonging to each family. Polygamy was common. Kinship ties were important, and the head of a family was owed great respect.

The houses were primarily places to sleep and store goods. Most activities took place outdoors. Farming and domestic work—cooking, fetching water and firewood, and similar tasks—generally fell to girls and women, although in many groups men cleared new fields for planting. The men were primarily hunters and warriors, and they also supervised the herds. Often boys were assigned to care for the cattle and milk them, with their work closely watched by older men.

Cattle were a mark of wealth; and this, coupled with growing population and continued migration from the north, meant that the Bantu-speaking groups were always expanding their territory to find pasture for their herds. Many of these tribes were loosely organized into small groups, each headed by a chief. Members of such a group might be related, but membership was determined by allegiance to the chief rather than blood ties. Thus a strong chief who attracted followers would find himself at the head of a growing group, while a weak chief might see his followers trickle away. When an area became crowded, a relative of a chief might form a new group and move on to settle in a new area. Sometimes this led to a civil war within the tribe; sometimes to conflict with a neighboring tribe. But in South Africa's early days, land was still plentiful. Tribal federations headed by strong chiefs developed in the 1700s and 1800s as conflict over land increased.

The chief's position was usually hereditary, passed on

from father to a son. As head of the tribe, he had great authority—and also immense responsibility for the welfare of his people. But in most cases he did not rule alone. Tribal councils (sometimes made up of the chief's close relatives; sometimes larger groups) usually aided in decision-making. At times a chief might turn for advice to a diviner, a person who was skilled in communication with the spirit world.

The Bantu-speaking groups had complex religious beliefs. Ancestor worship—the belief that the spirits of a person's ancestors lived on after death and could act to help or hinder the living—was important in most of the groups. In keeping with their respect for senior family members, many people believed that prayers and offerings to one's ancestors were necessary to avoid calamity. Most of the groups also shared a belief in an overriding spirit that ruled the universe. And there were often local spirits, in many cases sinister ones, as well. Through dreams and visions, the diviner was supposed to be able to see and speak with the ancestors and spirits, and to interpret their actions for ordinary people.

The descendants of the various Bantu-speaking tribes form the black population of South Africa today. They can be divided into four main groups, based on their languages, and into a number of subgroups. The largest group is the Nguni, who include four important subgroups: the Xhosa, the Zulu, the Swazi, and the Ndebele. In the Bantu migrations, the Nguni tribes spread down the east coast. By the 1600s, some Xhosa had reached the eastern Cape, while the Zulu were concentrated in what is now Natal. Most of the Ndebele settled farther north, in the areas that are today the eastern Transvaal and Zimbabwe.

The Sotho, the second of the four main groups, moved into the central regions of the country. The North Sotho settled in the Transvaal region, where they set up large, clustered villages surrounded by fields and pastures. The

South Sotho continued on to the areas that today are the Orange Free State and the tiny independent nation of Lesotho. The Tswana, a third Sotho subgroup, moved farther west, settling in the present-day area of Botswana as well as in South Africa.

The two remaining groups of the main four are the Venda and the Tsonga. Both were offshoots of East African groups. Fewer of these people settled in South Africa than did those of the other groups, and they were scattered in small villages in the east and north.

From the late 1400s on, each of these groups at one place or another began to come in contact with a new group—one that would eventually shatter their way of life. The new group was the white race: Europeans, who began to stop along Africa's coasts in their trading voyages to the Far East.

THE FIRST EUROPEANS

In 1488, the explorer Bartholomew Dias sailed from Portugal down the west coast of Africa in search of a route to the fabled riches of the Orient. He swung wide from the coast and rounded the tip of the continent without sighting it. Then he put in to the African shore twice, at Mossel Bay (about 200 miles [320 km] east of the Cape) and Algoa Bay (the site of modern Port Elizabeth), where he erected a pillar and a cross. At that point, a rebellious crew forced him to turn around and head for home. It was on the return voyage that he discovered the tip of Africa —a point he named Cape of Storms for the rough weather that buffeted his ship as he passed it. King John II of Portugal changed the name to Cape of Good Hope.

The fact that Dias had rounded the tip of Africa and discovered the Cape indeed raised hope that a route to the East would be found. Another Portuguese explorer, Vasco da Gama, returned in 1497 and also put in at Mossel Bay. There he met a group of Khoikhoi who welcomed the ship's crew and traded some of their cattle for ornaments. The Portuguese reported that the meeting was friendly; what the Khoikhoi thought of their visitors isn't known. Da Gama continued and reached India on this voyage, proving that a sea route from Europe to the East was possible. More Portuguese ships quickly followed, seizing ports along India's west coast in an effort to take control of the lucrative Eastern trade. But Dutch and British ships were not far behind.

Trading ships anchored often off the African coast to take on water and trade for food with black groups. By the 1520s Portugal had established bases in the west, in the area that is now Zaïre, and in the east, in present-day Mozambique and Zimbabwe. Relations between blacks and whites in these areas followed a general pattern: The two groups would be friendly at first, but soon violence would break out over some misunderstanding. Then the Portuguese would quickly conquer whatever black group was involved. In this way, the Portuguese bases were turned into colonies, and Portugal became involved in yet another kind of trade—slavery.

Throughout the 1500s, however, South Africa had only occasional contact with whites, and no white settlements were established. There were two reasons. One was the rough weather off the Cape of Good Hope, which made sailors eager to hurry around the continent's tip without stopping. The second was a reputation for unfriendly inhabitants. This reputation stemmed from an incident that took place in 1510 in which the viceroy, or governor, of Portuguese India stopped at Table Bay (near modern Cape Town) and was killed in a conflict with the Khoikhoi.

Neither storms nor a fearful reputation kept the traders away forever, however. In the 1600s, Portugal's sea power began to decline, while Britain's and the Netherlands' grew stronger. British ships stopped at Table Bay often in the early 1600s. In 1614, Britain's king James I sent convicts to Robben Island, a barren island just off

*Jan van Riebeeck, with other members
of the Dutch East India Company,
lands near present-day Cape Town in 1652.*

the coast of present-day Cape Town. (The island is still a prison, and in modern times many black dissidents have been held there.)

But it was the Dutch, not the British, who first arrived to stay. In 1647, the *Haarlem*, a ship belonging to the Dutch East India Company, was wrecked in Table Bay. The crew made it ashore and, while waiting to be picked up by the next passing ship, explored the area. They recommended it as a site for a refreshment station where Dutch ships on the India route could put in regularly and be assured of fresh water and supplies. Stops along the way were necessary because sailors often suffered from scurvy and other forms of malnutrition on the long trips to and from India.

Five years later, on April 6, 1652, Jan van Riebeeck led three Dutch East India Company ships to the site of present-day Cape Town to set up such a station. On board were just under a hundred people (all but four of them men)—South Africa's first white settlers. The stage was set for a conflict that would span three centuries and reach into modern times.

3

TAKING
THE LAND

The Dutch who founded Cape Town in 1652 didn't begin
with the idea of creating a colony and taking control of
the land. Their orders were to establish a "fort and garden," and the refreshment station they founded was just
that—a place where Dutch East India Company ships
could stop for fresh food and water. The settlers owned
no land themselves; all were employees of the trading
company. Well before the end of the century, however,
the picture had changed.

DUTCH EXPANSION

The first white settlers built their fort, marked out a few
fields, and traded with the Khoikhoi for cattle, which they
used to provision ships and to start small herds of their
own. The approximately fifteen thousand Khoikhoi in the
area welcomed the trade at first; the local San, who numbered about ten thousand, also accepted the whites. But as
time went on and it became clear that the newcomers were
there to stay, the Khoikhoi became less willing trading
partners. Their cattle were their livelihood, and they

weren't prepared to provide the Dutch with either the numbers or the quality they demanded. Relations deteriorated, each side accused the other of stealing cattle, and charges flew back and forth. The accusations culminated in violence in 1659, in a conflict later known as the First Hottentot War. The Khoikhoi took the worst of the fight, and the Cape Town settlement expanded its frontiers.

That scenario was to be replayed again and again over the following years as repeated clashes gave the Dutch not only land but thousands of Khoikhoi cattle and sheep. Meanwhile, other changes were taking place in the Cape Town settlement. For one thing, the settlers had little taste for manual labor, and they needed servants to help run their households, raise their crops, and care for their cattle. The Khoikhoi and the San, with their free and nomadic way of life, had no taste for this work. Thus, within a few years of its founding, Cape Town began to import slaves. Some were blacks brought from farther north in Africa; more were from the Dutch East Indies—from Sumatra, Java, the Celebes Islands—and from India itself. As in the American South, slavery was established along racial lines. The dry climate and lack of good farmland in most of the country helped prevent South Africa from ever developing the type of huge plantations that were a feature of the American South. But slaves, usually a few to a household, were a feature of everyday life there for the next 175 years.

A second change in the settlement—and one that seems surprising in light of South Africa's later history—was racial mixing. The fact that most of the original Cape settlers were men inevitably led to this. The white settlers, the majority of whom were soldiers and sailors, were cut off from their homeland, so they took wives from the East Indian, black, and Khoikhoi groups. This racial mixing gave rise to the group that is known as coloured in South Africa today. The coloureds are still concentrated around Cape Town and include a subgroup, the Cape Malays, who trace their ancestry more directly to East Indian slaves.

Mixed marriages didn't mean that these other racial groups were considered the equals of whites. Van Riebeeck, for one, termed the Khoikhoi a "dull, rude, lazy, and stinking nation." But the children of the early mixed marriages were not always entirely looked down upon—that came later, as racial attitudes hardened. Custom, rather than law, made them a separate group; some who acquired education and wealth even achieved the status of whites. Even today, while racial categories are supposedly set by law, lines between racial groups are blurred. Many Afrikaners (whites of Dutch descent) have a touch of coloured ancestry somewhere in their family trees, and many coloureds are indistinguishable from whites. The confusion results in a certain number of people being "reclassified," or arbitrarily switched from one racial category to another, each year.

A third change in the settlement stemmed from dissatisfaction with the rule of the Dutch East India Company. The governor ruled by decree; as one historian of the time put it, "the caprice of the governor was in truth the law." Some settlers chafed at this rule and longed to start their own farms, as independent landholders rather than company employees. In 1657, the governor gave in, allotted them land, and allowed them to set up as independent burghers, or citizens. These settlers became known as the *Boers*, a Dutch word meaning "farmers."

The company found the experiment in free farming successful—the Boers were a more reliable source of cattle and foodstuffs than the Khoikhoi. Thus, about twenty years after the first Boer farms were established, the settlement was opened to newcomers. The company offered land, burgher status, and free passage to anyone who would make the voyage, and it had many takers. Not only Dutch but German settlers flowed in. In 1688, a new group began to arrive: the French Protestants known as Huguenots, who were fleeing religious persecution in their home country. Many were from wine-producing regions in France, and they planted vineyards in South Africa.

Thus the Cape refreshment station began to grow into a Dutch colony. Although the settlers came from many countries, the government did its best to blend them into a unified society. And, for the most part, it succeeded. The Huguenots, for example, weren't allowed to settle in one area; they were scattered among Dutch farms throughout the Cape. Dutch was the official language, and it gradually developed into Afrikaans, the language spoken by descendants of the early settlers today. The Dutch Reformed Church, a Protestant denomination, was established throughout the colony.

Schools and the other social services we take for granted today were limited or nonexistent. Most of the settlers who came to establish farms lived hard and isolated lives. Education consisted of Bible readings. Fiercely independent in spirit, these people saw themselves more and more as a group chosen by God to tame the wilderness. Meanwhile, their independent nature often brought them in conflict with the government in Cape Town. They resented the rules set by the Dutch East India Company, which controlled all trade, and often broke them by trading illegally with the Khoikhoi or with passing ships.

By 1700, whites occupied most of the good farmland around Cape Town and were spilling over into the drier regions to the north and east. Here, where poor soil and uncertain weather made farming difficult, they more often turned from crop growing to ranching. And as their herds of sheep and cattle grew, they needed more and more land for pasture. Some even adopted a seminomadic way of life, staying in an area until the pasture was used up and then packing up their families and their belongings to move on. To supplement their livings, they killed game.

These *trekboers*, as the ranchers were called, were at the forefront of conflicts with the Khoikhoi and the San—conflicts that increased as the colony gradually spread. The Boers raided Khoikhoi cattle, and the Khoikhoi raided Boer cattle. Even the San, seeing the desirability of keep-

An artist's rendition of Dutch colonists offering the Khoikhoi a variety of implements in trade for cattle

ing herds of animals, began to accumulate cattle and sheep and were often involved in raids. The Boers' racial attitudes hardened: The Khoikhoi and San were their rivals for control of the land and therefore enemies.

But these people, with their essentially Stone Age cultures, were no match for the whites and their guns—or for the Europeans' diseases. In 1713 an epidemic of smallpox, brought by a ship en route from India, killed a quarter of the white population and virtually wiped out the Khoikhoi. Those who were left were in no position to resist the advance of white settlement. They were mostly reduced to the status of servants to whites. To the Boers, the Khoikhoi were now a conquered people and little better than slaves. A master's command was law; servants did as they were told or often faced harsh punishment.

The San, meanwhile, fared no better. From 1715 to 1774, there were five major and countless minor clashes between the San and the whites. The San were hunted like wild animals, and in 1792 the government even set a bounty on them, including women and children as fair game. Sometimes white farmers armed their Khoikhoi servants to help in the hunt. To survive, the dwindling numbers of San retreated farther and farther into the remote, dry regions of the northwest. The few who remain today live mostly in the area of the Kalahari Desert.

As they traveled east, the *trekboers* also met southern-moving Bantu-speaking groups, whom they lumped together under the name "kaffirs" (now considered an insulting term). The Xhosa, southernmost of the groups, were the first to make contact. The first minor clash is reported to have taken place in 1702; in 1736, Boers fought with a group of Xhosa 350 miles (560 km) east of Table Bay. By the 1770s, white settlement had grown beyond the area of present-day Port Elizabeth to the Fish River. The river served as a dividing line between the whites and the Xhosa, and for a while the two groups were able to trade peacefully.

But the concept of private land ownership was foreign

to the Xhosa, and they freely crossed the border to pasture their herds. Charges of cattle stealing were traded back and forth. In the First Kaffir War, in 1779, the Xhosa were driven back beyond the Fish River and lost some five thousand cattle to the whites. The Fish was again set as a boundary between the two groups, but the agreement allowed the Xhosa to cross it. This angered some of the Boers, and incidents of violence continued. In 1789, fighting broke out again. The Xhosa were driven farther east, to the Buffalo River.

These first conflicts with the Xhosa set a pattern that would be repeated again and again as the whites expanded their territory. Neither culture understood the ways of the other. Both needed the land, and the whites were the more powerful of the two. Just as the United States expanded westward through a series of wars and broken agreements with the American Indians, the whites of South Africa moved eastward at the expense of the Xhosa and, later, other Bantu-speaking groups. Unlike the San, however, these groups weren't driven into remote areas. Rather, they were compressed into ever-shrinking territories— territories too limited to support their population.

While the Boers were fighting the Xhosa on the eastern frontier, the atmosphere in the Cape Town area was charged with talk of human rights. But in these discussions, it was not black rights that were in question: By this time, racist attitudes had hardened to the point where blacks were considered lesser beings, condemned (as one writer put it) "by Almighty God to servitude and abuse." Rather, it was white rights that were under discussion. Fueled by news of the American Revolution and by the talk of rights that was common in many European countries in the late 1700s, Cape Town burghers were demanding more say in government and a greater share in trading profits. The government offered only token reforms, and the rebellious mood spread out into the countryside. Farmers in two settlements east of Cape Town, Swellendam and Graaf Reinet, rebelled in 1795 and attempted to set up their own republic. Among their complaints was the government's refusal to decree that all San and Khoikhoi were automatically slaves and could be punished as their masters saw fit.

It was at that point that British warships sailed into Table Bay to take control of the colony.

THE BRITISH

The events that prompted the British arrival took place far away from South Africa, in Europe. In the aftermath of the French Revolution of 1789, wars and conflicts tore the continent. Holland's ruler, the Prince of Orange, was forced out by a French-supported party. He fled to England (which opposed France) and asked the British to take control of his overseas possessions and hold them for him. The transfer of control was orderly and peaceful. The British returned the colony to the Dutch in 1803, but three years later new wars broke out in Europe and the British reclaimed it. The Cape Colony was permanently ceded to the British in 1814, and the first major British settlement was founded near Port Elizabeth in 1820.

Among the first changes the British made were economic reforms that gave the burghers more trading rights. This helped quiet the mood of dissent in the colony. Other British changes were less popular, however: The new government banned the importation of slaves and abolished some brutal forms of capital punishment. In 1809, the British also set about writing laws that, for the first time, would define the relationship between master and servant in the colony.

In effect, these laws merely confirmed the practices that were already common and encouraged blacks to become servants of whites. The Khoikhoi were required to have fixed residences, forbidden to own land, and barred from moving from one district to another without a pass. Any nonwhite captured in a raid could be declared an "apprentice" and forced into a long period of servitude, a situation that encouraged the Boers on the frontiers to attack black groups in the hope of carrying off women and children. A nonwhite child born while his or her parents were in service and raised to the age of eight was required to serve as an apprentice until the age of eighteen. In short, the laws placed such heavy restrictions on black servants that they were little more than slaves.

The laws cut two ways, however. They also required minimum standards of treatment for slaves and servants and limited the brutality with which they could be punished. This sat ill with some of the Boers, who resented British interference in what they considered private matters. In 1815 a white farmer defied an order to answer charges that he had mistreated blacks, and he was killed while resisting police who came to arrest him. The event sparked a Boer revolt; the British crushed it and hanged five of the leaders at Slachter's Nek. But the result of the affair was a growing bitterness between the Boers and the British.

Pressure for better treatment of blacks came from another source. Not long after the new government was in place, the London Missionary Society and other, similar groups had begun to arrive. These groups were appalled by the conditions they found among the Khoikhoi, and they began to set up mission communities that gave the Khoikhoi education and an option—a chance to be something other than servants to whites. The missionaries rejected the view that the Khoikhoi were fated to live in "servitude and abuse." On the contrary. One of their most important leaders, John Philip, said, "The natural capacity of the Africans is nothing inferior to that of the Europeans."

The pleadings of the missionaries were well received in London, and the British made major changes. In 1828, most of the restrictions on the Khoikhoi—the pass laws, mandatory apprenticing of children, and long work contracts—were abolished. In 1834, all slaves (they numbered about forty thousand) were freed. The Boers, unhappy with the money they received for their slaves and seeing their hold over their servants weakened, resented the British even more. They also objected to the fact that English, rather than their native Dutch, had become the language used in courts and schools.

The last straw for the Boers was the conflict with the Xhosa on the eastern frontier. Fighting had continued, with British troops called in to protect the eastern farmers. In 1834 the Cape Colony entered its sixth major war with the Xhosa and pushed them back beyond the Kei River. All Xhosa land southwest of the Kei was ceded to whites. But in London, missionary groups protested that the Xhosa's land was being taken from them unfairly. The British reversed the decree and gave the disputed land back to the Xhosa—and the Boers' resentment reached the boiling point.

The atmosphere in the Cape Colony was not unlike that in the United States at that time, where North and South had begun to split on the issue of slavery. Certainly the Boers' feelings about the British reforms equalled the Southerners' feelings about Northern reform movements —the changes seemed to strike at what they saw as the God-given order of the world, which placed blacks clearly beneath whites. In the United States, the conflict led ulti- mately to civil war. But the Boers' situation and their way of life was different from that of the Southerners. They had no political power and no hope of defeating the British army in a revolt. They also hadn't built up large planta- tions that depended on slaves.

Instead of rebelling, then, those who were most strongly anti-British did something that, with their history, made more sense: From 1835 to about 1837, they packed their belongings into wagons and moved out in large groups beyond the colony's borders, heading north and northeast. This was the Great Trek, a central event in white South African history. The Boers who left became known as Voortrekkers.

Ironically, many of the developments that so incensed the Boers were short-lived. Slavery never returned, but tough new master and servant laws were imposed in the Cape Colony in 1841. While these laws made no reference to color, they had their greatest effect on black servants and established stiff penalties for such "crimes" as disobedience and insolence to a master. Likewise, the land that was returned to the Xhosa in 1834 was under black control for only a few more years. From 1845 to 1846, drought and an attack of locusts heated up the struggle for grazing lands, and the British took back the disputed land in another war.

Fighting broke out again in 1850, and although it cost the British £2 million to defeat the Xhosa, they took still more land. A new British governor, Sir George Grey, began a program designed to teach blacks skills and crafts in the hope of incorporating them into the colony. But the Xhosa valued their independent way of life, and quarrels over land continued.

The heaviest blow for the Xhosa was yet to come. Pressed by the white advance, they turned to their gods. In 1856, Mhlakaza, a diviner and counselor to the Xhosa chief Kreli, prophesied that the dead Xhosa would come to life to aid the living in their struggle, and all whites would be swept away by a great wind. First, however, a great sacrifice was required: All the Xhosa cattle must be killed, all crops destroyed, and nothing planted. The Xhosa followed his instructions to the letter and waited for the miracle to arrive on the appointed day—February 18, 1857. But no miracle arrived, and in the months that followed more than thirty thousand Xhosa died of starvation. The remaining Xhosa were forced to beg from the whites.

The cattle killing, as the incident is known, was in keeping with the Xhosa religious beliefs—the belief that ancestors could intervene to aid the living. That a great

sacrifice was required seemed only fitting. But the cattle killing was also a desperate act of resistance, the act of a people who had been pushed to the limit and saw their way of life disintegrating. It failed. With the Xhosa population vastly reduced, stretches of empty land fell into white hands. Twenty years later, Chief Kreli managed to rally his people for a minor revolt, but they were quickly defeated. White possession of the Xhosa lands was assured.

NATAL AND THE ZULU

The lands beyond the Cape Colony's borders were not empty, and as the Boers moved out it was inevitable that they would come in conflict with larger and more powerful black groups. The most feared of these were the Zulu, who were concentrated in the area that is now Natal.

Beginning in the late 1700s, the Zulu had united under a series of strong chiefs. Dingiswayo, the first of these, introduced some new battle techniques such as fighting in formation (perhaps picked up from the Europeans) and organized a powerful army. The next chief, Shaka, went further. Taking firm control over Zulu society, he claimed all of Natal as his empire and trained his warriors in vicious hand-to-hand fighting with a new weapon, a short stabbing spear. Shaka's armies threw the region into a state of upheaval—since defeat at his hands meant death or at best enslavement, other black groups fell back before him. They were squeezed by the Zulu on one side and by advancing whites on the other. Some tribes escaped to the north and northwest. Others were entirely wiped out, and great areas of land were laid waste. In later years this period of wars and migrations became known as mfeqane, or "the upheaval."

Boers negotiate rugged terrain during the Great Trek in 1835.

Ultimately Shaka was killed by his half brother, Dingane, who took over the kingdom. He was in power when the first Voortrekkers reached Natal in 1838. The Voortrekkers attempted to make a deal with Dingane for land, but instead his warriors murdered a group of three hundred whites and two hundred and fifty Khoikhoi servants. The whites got the worst of it in several subsequent fights, too, until on December 16, 1838, they mustered reinforcements and met the Zulu at Blood River. The Voortrekkers numbered five hundred, against some ten thousand Zulu. But, led by Andries Pretorius, they circled their wagons (or formed a *laager*) and killed some three thousand Zulu while suffering only three casualties of their own. The guns of the whites were the deciding factor in the battle. But, true to their self-image as a chosen people, the Boers attributed the victory to divine intervention.

Although they continued to control an independent territory (Zululand) in the north of Natal for another fifty years, the Zulu's power was broken. Dingane escaped with some of his forces but was finally defeated the following year. He fled to what is now Swaziland, where he was captured and tortured to death by one of the many tribal enemies he had made during his career.

The Boers settled in on the land they had won from the Zulu and established Natalia, a republic. Within its borders they set aside reserves for blacks and barred them from traveling outside these areas. But, since they also needed labor, they set up an "apprenticeship" system in which black children were required to serve to the age of twenty-one (for women) or twenty-five (for men). To get apprentices (and livestock), they freely raided the Zulu and other tribes in the area.

But Natalia was to be short-lived. Some of the tribes complained to the British about the Boer raids. As a result, the British invaded Natalia in 1842 and annexed it the following year. The Voortrekkers moved on, headed toward the region of modern Johannesburg. The British eventually extended their rule over the region in 1887 when they annexed Zululand. But meanwhile, they set up a system of government in Natal that was to have a strong influence on South Africa's later policies toward blacks.

Under this system, whites and blacks were ruled separately. Tribal units were restored and chiefs were appointed. British commissioners oversaw the chiefs, and a British governor was given the title of supreme chief, with power over all blacks. A separate code of laws was also adopted for blacks, combining African tribal law with British interpretations. A "civilized" black could apply for, and perhaps receive, exemption from this separate law, but most blacks fell under it. The British also imposed master and servant laws, similar to those in the Cape Colony.

British settlers soon moved into Natal, and many of them established large sugar plantations along the coast. And, beginning in the 1860s, a new group of people began arriving in Natal. They were Indians, brought as indentured servants to work the plantations—work that the Zulu had refused to do. Their usual term of service was five years. But they were allowed to remain if they wished, and many did. Natal's Indian community grew until, by the end of the century, Indians outnumbered whites and formed a separate class, midway in status between blacks and whites.

THE BOER REPUBLICS

While the British, the Boers, and the Zulu were fighting over Natal, other Voortrekkers headed toward the regions that are now the Orange Free State and the Transvaal, acquiring land by barter, conquest, and sometimes a combination of the two. Because tribal boundaries were unclear and because the northern regions were in a state of flux and upheaval, it was not always certain who held what land. On at least one occasion, the Voortrekkers bartered for land with one group only to find that it was in fact held by another—a misunderstanding that prompted a bloody battle. The Boers were often ruthless in their dealings with blacks, however. In one incident, a hunting party of twenty-odd whites, out looking for "apprentices," were killed by blacks. In revenge, whites attacked the tribe and killed nine hundred. When the rest fled to nearby caves, the whites sat outside and shot anyone who came out. A tribe of two thousand people was completely wiped out by bullets or thirst within a month.

On their way north, the Boers passed through a strip of small "treaty states" that the British had established along the Orange River, at the Cape Colony's northern borders. These states, formed in the early 1800s, were meant to serve as buffers between the colony and the up-heavals and migrations of black groups in the north. Among them were Griqualand, founded by a group of free coloureds under the leadership of Adam Kok, a former slave; and Basutoland, a Sotho tribal state under the rule of Chief Moshweshwe. In exchange for their buffer role, these states had been promised British friendship and support.

Some of the Boers settled in the treaty states—but they didn't always recognize the States' sovereignty or their laws. As a result, there was friction. In 1845, for example, Kok attempted to arrest a white for flogging his black servants, and fighting broke out in Griqualand. The British worked out a compromise that left many of the Griquas unhappy—half of their land was reserved for them, and half was to be leased to whites. Two years later, with con-flict continuing, Britain formally annexed most of the treaty states. Each was left with a form of self-government but was placed under the authority of a British resident, or governor. In practice, the British were careful not to let any of the states' rulers become too powerful. For example, the British resident encouraged dissidents in the Basuto tribe so that Moshweshwe would not become too strong.

The Boers in the region, finding themselves under the same government they had tried to escape, revolted. The revolt was put down, but it resulted in an agreement—the Sand River Convention of 1852—in which the British promised not to interfere with the Boers north of the Vaal River, which today forms part of the boundary between the Orange Free State and the Transvaal. Nor was Britain anxious to maintain its rule in the troubled region between the Orange and the Vaal rivers. In 1854, it ceded the land to the Boers, who formed the Orange Free State Republic at Bloemfontein.

It was not long before new fighting broke out. During the time of "the upheaval," when Zulu war parties had thrown the region into turmoil, Moshweshwe had led his people east into the Drakensberg Mountains to avoid defeat by the Zulu. The Boers now claimed that by abandoning territory, the Basuto had forfeited their claims to all the land between the Orange and the Vaal. From 1856 to 1868, the Basuto and the Boers fought over the land. Finally the British intervened and, over Boer protests, fixed Basutoland's borders. Basutoland became a separate British colony. Today it is the nation of Lesotho.

North of the Vaal, in the Transvaal, the Voortrekkers had established the South African Republic in 1844, with its capital at Pretoria (named for Andries Pretorius, the hero of Blood River). Here, after the 1852 Sand River Convention, they faced no interference from the British. Internal bickering plagued the new republic, however, and it went through several constitutions and leaders. One thing that Boers in the Transvaal and the Orange Free State agreed on, however, was the position of blacks in society. Nonwhites could not hold property, could not get married, and most certainly could not vote. Anyone with a fraction of nonwhite blood was excluded from the political process, and laws clearly spelled out the government policy of "no equality . . . in Church or State."

Thus, by the 1860s, South Africa was divided into

British and Afrikaner regions, with only a few areas remaining under black or coloured control. The blacks had been deprived of most of their land and pushed into small enclaves—areas that were increasingly too small to support them. Those who remained in white-controlled regions, even the more lenient British areas, were denied equal treatment and lived essentially as servants and laborers.

Then, in 1867, came an event that would have a profound impact on South Africa's future. A farmer strolling near Hopetown, on the banks of the Orange River, stopped to watch a group of children playing "marbles" with water-washed stones from the river. One of the stones shone more brightly than the others. It was a diamond.

4

DIAMONDS
AND GOLD

The diamond found on the banks of the Orange River in
1867 was just the first of many. Over the next three years,
more were found to the north, in the area of Kimberley.
The Kimberley diamond field, in fact, turned out to be
one of the world's richest sources of these precious stones.

But it was soon apparent that South Africa's mineral
wealth extended far beyond this single area. There were
diamonds in Orange Free State, too, and in 1872 gold was
discovered in eastern Transvaal. More gold discoveries
followed—including, in 1886, the discovery of vast deposits
on the Witwatersrand. To the white powers, two things
now became enormously important: ownership of the land
where the rich minerals lay and control of the labor that
would bring them to the surface.

THE RUSH FOR WEALTH

The Kimberley diamond area lay near the boundaries of
three states—Transvaal, Orange Free State, and a Griqua
(free coloured) territory that had so far remained independent. All three, as well as several Tswana groups,

claimed it. The Griquas, to get support from the Cape Colony in their claim, agreed to let their territory be annexed by the British. The dispute over the diamond fields was settled without fighting. The lieutenant governor of Natal, the only South African region not involved, set up a commission that made the decision: The diamond fields went to the Griquas and were promptly annexed by the Cape Colony. Soon the British and others were pouring into the region to establish mines that they hoped would make them wealthy beyond their dreams.

Once gold was discovered in the Transvaal, the British thought twice about the agreement they had made in the 1852 Sand River Convention not to interfere north of the Vaal River. Land that had once been of little value—and full of danger from marauding black groups—suddenly became extremely desirable. The British looked for an opening that would allow them to move into the area. They thought they found one—in the Boers' continued arguments among themselves and in their fights with black groups.

By the mid-1870s, the internal divisions in the Afrikaner republics had heated up. Perhaps because of the fiercely independent nature that had prompted the Voortrekkers to head north in the first place, they seemed unable to agree on anything in politics or religion. Marthinus Pretorius, the son of Andries and the first president in the South African Republic, had tried to unify the various factions and groups but had failed. He left to take the post of president in the Orange Free State in 1859 (he returned to the Transvaal to serve another brief turn as president ten years later). Presidents who followed had no better success. Disputes reached such a point that in 1874 a group of dissatisfied farmers hitched up their wagons and headed off again, into the deserts to the northwest. Many died, and only a fragment of the group finally reached Portuguese West Africa, where they settled.

At the same time that their internal disputes over politics and religion were raging, the Boers were fighting running conflicts with black groups in the area. These fights and continued political squabbles kept the Transvaal from becoming strong, either militarily or economically. This was the opening the British saw. In 1877, claiming that the Boers' inability to end black unrest posed a threat to British colonies farther south, they announced their intention to annex the Transvaal. First, they began a campaign for Afrikaner support, promising the Boers a separate legislature, stable government, and an immediate loan of one hundred thousand pounds. As much as the Afrikaner factions disliked each other, however, they disliked the British more. So, when Britain saw that support was not forthcoming, it annexed the Transvaal anyway, by decree.

But, for the British, the timing was wrong. Not long after the decree, they found themselves embroiled in their ninth (and last) war with the Xhosa, in the southeast, and with a major Zulu rebellion in Natal. The Afrikaners saw an opportunity: The British forces were spread too thin. The Transvaal Afrikaners rebelled in 1880, setting off the First Boer War. Realizing their predicament, the British made peace the following year. They granted the Afrikaners self-government and the right to set their own policies toward blacks, although they retained control of foreign affairs.

Conflict with the British helped draw the quarreling Afrikaners closer together, and in 1883 a strong new Afrikaner leader emerged—Stephanus Paul Kruger. As president of the Transvaal, he won even more concessions and territory from the British. He also established a pass system for blacks, which forbade them to move from one area to another without specific permission. Afrikaner power seemed on the rise. A group of Afrikaners even backed a new outbreak of rebellion among the Zulu in 1884. In exchange for their help, they took half of Zululand; the British, alarmed, quickly annexed the rest. This brought white control of the land up to the Limpopo River, which today forms South Africa's northeastern border.

But Afrikaner power did not grow unchecked. Especially after major gold deposits were discovered on the Witwatersrand in 1886, outsiders—*uitlanders,* as the Afrikaners called them—flooded into the Transvaal in the hope of making a fortune. Within ten years of the Witwatersrand find, three-fourths of the Transvaal whites were *uitlanders,* most of them British. Kruger, intent on keeping power in Afrikaner hands, denied the *uitlanders* (as well as the blacks) the right to vote, and they became increasingly angry.

The man who brought matters to a head was Cecil John Rhodes, a British subject who had come to South Africa for his health (he had had tuberculosis), opened a diamond mine at Kimberley in 1871, and gradually increased his holdings until he was one of the richest men in the Cape Colony—indeed, in the world. Ultimately he combined his holdings to form De Beers Consolidated Mines, still the world's largest diamond producer.

Rhodes was not only wealthy; he was powerful. He had a dream of British colonial rule spreading across all of Africa, and he set about making it a reality. He was elected to the Cape assembly in 1881 and pressed for British annexation of the area that is now Zimbabwe (formerly named Rhodesia, after him). He became prime minister of the Cape in 1890 and began to plan a great rail route that would span the full length of Africa, from the Cape to Cairo. But right on the Cape Colony's doorstep there was an obstacle to this sweeping plan of British dominance—the Afrikaner republics.

As a private citizen, Rhodes also had gold-mining interests in the Transvaal; using that toehold, he developed a plan that, he hoped, would bring the British to power. First he had some of his henchmen stir up unrest among the *uitlanders,* getting them to agitate for voting and other

*Cecil Rhodes, seated on ground at right,
built an empire in South Africa.*

rights. Then, in 1895, acting on his orders, Rhodesian troops staged a raid on the Transvaal that he expected would set off a revolt and oust the Afrikaners from power. This attack, the Jameson Raid, was botched, and Rhodes's plan failed. He was criticized so severely that he was forced to resign as prime minister.

But the unrest Rhodes had helped stir up did not die down. With a little additional stirring by Alfred Milner, the new Cape Colony governor, it increased until in 1899 the *uitlanders* asked Britain for help. Britain tried to negotiate with the Afrikaner government, but the talks produced nothing. Fighting broke out in October 1899 when the Orange Free State joined the South African Republic in declaring war on Britain.

THE ANGLO-BOER WAR
AND ITS AFTERMATH

The British thought they would settle the dispute in a short and decisive campaign—there was talk of peace by Christmas. In fact, the war was to drag on for two and a half bitter years. The British poured troops into the fight. Led by Lord Roberts and Lord Kitchener, a total of 450,000 British and colonial soldiers were sent into combat, and 20,000 died. They faced a far smaller and far weaker Afrikaner force under the command of General Louis Botha—about 87,000 commandos and irregulars (7,000 of whom were killed), basically farmers turned soldiers. The Boers used black servants as scouts, drivers, and laborers. They were shocked when the British armed some blacks for combat roles (although, even in the British army, blacks were not on an equal footing with whites).

The early victories went to the Boers. The second week of December became known as the "Black Week" for the British; they met with defeat in three major battles at Magersfontein, Stormberg, and Colenso. Early in 1900, however, the British brought in more troops, and by mid-

The Battery and Balloon Corps of the
British Army under Lord Roberts advances
on Johannesburg during the Boer War.

June they had succeeded in capturing the capitals of both Afrikaner states. Botha's main army surrendered to the British in September 1900. But the rest of the Afrikaner forces took to the hills and carried on a guerrilla campaign, hanging on with the dogged independence and determination that had marked all their previous history.

More devastating than any specific battle was the effect of the fighting on the countryside. In an attempt to cut off support for the guerrillas, the British pursued a scorched earth policy: As they moved into Afrikaner territory, they looted and razed farms; slaughtered cattle, sheep, and horses; and rounded up women and children for imprisonment in concentration camps. Conditions in the camps were so bad that more than twenty thousand prisoners died of disease, malnutrition, and neglect. When word of this ongoing tragedy reached England, it produced a scandal, and conditions at the camps were improved so that the death rate slowed. But another scandal was not unearthed until later: The British had also rounded up the Afrikaners' black servants for internment, and conditions in the separate black camps were even worse. Untold thousands of blacks died before the end of the war.

The last guerrilla forces surrendered in May 1902. Under the Treaty of Vereeniging, signed in Pretoria later that month, the two defeated Boer states—the Orange Free State and the Transvaal—became British colonies. But the British terms were not harsh: All prisoners were allowed to return to their homes, no one was punished for taking part in the war, and the Afrikaner territories were to have a measure of self-government and their own legislatures. To avoid inflaming Afrikaner feelings, no mention was made of the status of blacks under the new arrangement. Essentially, blacks had no status—the Anglo-Boer War had been a fight between whites for control of the land, control that had already been wrested from blacks in earlier battles.

*This Boer gun team saw
action against the British.*

CONTROLLING LABOR

The four units that now made up Britain's South African colonies—Cape Colony, Natal, Orange Free State, and Transvaal—each had different policies toward nonwhites. In part, these policies reflected different views about the relationship of whites and nonwhites. In part, they reflected different needs for labor.

In the Cape, still largely a farming region, blacks and coloureds theoretically had a qualified vote since the 1850s. In practice, however, few of them actually voted. The Cape constitution of 1892 decreed that anyone who owned property worth seventy-five pounds and could sign his name and write his address and occupation could cast a ballot in elections—but most blacks had little education and less property, and there was no great push to provide more. Although nonwhites were a majority of the population, they made up less than 15 percent of the voters. Only 3 percent of coloureds were registered; even so, coloured voters outnumbered black voters two to one. The situation was like that in the U.S. South after the Civil War when poll taxes and literacy requirements prevented many blacks from exercising their right to vote.

In Natal, too, there were no specific color restrictions on the vote. But an 1896 law denied the vote to people whose country of origin did not have "representative institutions founded on the parliamentary franchise"—that is, a democratic, parliamentary government. That ruled out most Indians. While those born in South Africa could vote in parliamentary and local elections, at the turn of the century there were only two hundred registered Indian voters. As whites felt more competition from the growing Indian community in the early 1900s, they placed new restrictions on Indians, too—denying them the right to buy land, refusing to issue them trading licenses, requiring them to pay special taxes, and placing additional restrictions on their right to vote. The goal was to pressure Indians into moving back to India; but for the most part, the Indians stayed.

Natal blacks were also considered outside the democratic tradition. This was reflected in the separate legal system that the British had set up earlier, based on tribal patterns. In the British view, whites were essentially trustees, overseeing black interests until some distant time when the blacks would be educated and "civilized" enough to take matters into their own hands. Until then, as one British colonial put it, it was "preposterous" and "unnatural" to talk of equality "between people so utterly dissimilar in civilization." Blacks made up less than one percent of Natal voters.

In the meantime, however, the nonwhites of Cape Colony and Natal provided a valuable pool of cheap labor for whites. One of the principal ways of encouraging blacks to enter white service was the "hut tax," first adopted in Natal in the 1850s. The tax was assessed on each black household. Since blacks who followed their traditional way of life raised only enough food for their own needs and had no hope of accumulating extra money, they were forced to work for whites for at least part of the year to pay it. Blacks who had had contact with the missions did not need such coercion because they had come to value labor and money. But, regardless, when they entered white service the British master and servant laws ensured obedience by providing stiff penalties for insolence.

The Afrikaners of the Transvaal and the Orange Free State viewed relations between whites and nonwhites even more severely. Nonwhites, in their eyes, had a clear and God-given role: They were "hewers of wood and drawers of water." Kruger, in 1882, had described the relationship this way: "The savages must be kept within bounds and always overruled by justice and morality." In accordance with this view, blacks and coloureds had no rights in the Afrikaner territories—they were not citizens, could not vote or own land, and could travel only with a pass issued by the white government. The Orange Free State forbade Indians to enter at all.

Like some of the laws governing blacks in the British areas, the stern Afrikaner restrictions on blacks had a practical root as well as a philosophical one. The Transvaal gold reserves were vast, but the ore was of low quality. That meant that to produce a given quantity of pure gold, much crude ore had to be mined. The mines, then, could turn a profit only if a supply of cheap labor was assured. By binding the blacks into strict labor contracts and forbidding them to travel freely, white mine owners were able to set up a situation that was ideal for their purposes. As one mine spokesman, arguing for stiff laws in the late 1900s, put it, the laws were necessary "to hold onto the native whom we have brought down at a considerable expense to ourselves."

The mine owners of this time also found a justification for the low wages they paid their workers. Blacks, they said, were incapable of looking into the future—they lived only for the moment. As soon as a black worker had a little money in his pocket, he would be certain to quit his job and head back to his reserve. So low wages were a necessity; they ensured that the workers would stay on the job longer.

The mine owners who took these views were by no means all Afrikaners—many British owners agreed. In fact, conditions at the British-owned Kimberley diamond mines in the 1880s were among the most severe of any. Workers were confined to a compound that was virtually a prison and required to work for at least four months straight, without a day off. They bought their food from a mining-company store and had no opportunity to see their families. With work conditions like these, it was not surprising that many blacks were eager to leave mine work at the first possible moment.

Thus, when the British took control of the Afrikaner states, they made no attempt to impose the more liberal, Cape Colony view of nonwhite rights. They were leery of inflaming Afrikaner feelings on the issue, and they recognized that a liberal view would work against their interests in the mines. That didn't mean there was no debate on the issue, however. In the early 1900s, the four separate units began to hold talks on the possibility of forming a union, and race was a major topic. Cape delegates to the talks insisted on maintaining nonwhite rights in their province, and they won the fight. But they were unable to convince the other delegates—particularly the hard-line Afrikaner representatives—that these rights should be extended throughout South Africa.

Recognizing that agreement on the issue was impossible, the Union of South Africa was set up in 1910 with each of the four provinces retaining its own separate policy where nonwhites were concerned. The Union was under British control only in the sense that it recognized the British sovereign as head of state and was a member of the British Commonwealth. In all else, it was self-governing, controlling its affairs through a powerful national parliament made up of two houses, the Senate and the House of Assembly. Although, theoretically, nonwhites could vote in the Cape, seats in Parliament were reserved for whites.

The Union's first prime minister, the former Boer War general Louis Botha, was a moderate Afrikaner who believed in cooperating with the British. All the same, pressure on nonwhites increased in the years following the founding of the Union. The first parliament, meeting in 1913, set up tribal reserves and formally forbade blacks—except those in the Cape—from buying land outside them. The new law forced thousands to pack their belongings and move off farms they had thought they owned. Blacks then made up 78 percent of the population; the reserves made up just slightly more than 7 percent of the land.

Writing some thirty-five years later, Alan Paton described in *Cry, the Beloved Country* the disastrous result this policy had on the land in black areas: "Too many cattle feed upon the grass, and too many fires have burned it. Stand shod upon it, for it is coarse and sharp, and the stones cut under the feet. . . . The great red hills stand desolate, and the earth has torn away like flesh. The lightning flashes over them, the clouds pour down upon them, the dead streams come to life, full of the red blood of the earth. Down in the valleys women scratch the soil that is left, and the maize hardly reaches the height of a man."

There were other restrictions in the new Union, too, many of them designed to ensure a supply of black labor for the mines: tight laws against vagrants and squatters who set up homes on open land, higher taxes on blacks, a ban on strikes by contract workers. The Union government also adopted the first of the industrial "color bar" laws, designed to keep blacks well down the social ladder. This law, passed in 1911, required skilled mining and engineering workers to get a government certificate, and blacks could not apply. Later, the law was extended to include other skills—engine driving, blasting, and surveying, for example. In theory, both white and coloured workers could be licensed for these jobs. But in practice, only whites got the certificates. The result was that nonwhites, forced to work as laborers, were prevented from ever advancing into skilled trades or management.

The situation in South Africa in the early 1900s, then, was one of legalized racial discrimination. It was more severe in some places than in others; there were whites who deplored it, and nonwhites who protested it. But—in contrast to the United States, where racial discrimination was officially condemned but existed nonetheless—here it was the law of the land. Discriminatory laws suited the belief in white supremacy that had marked white relations with blacks from the beginning. And they brought the full exploitation of South Africa's minerals within reach.

5

APARTHEID
ESTABLISHED

Among the many points of view that marked debate on racial policy in the early days of the Union, one was to emerge to shape the future of the country. This was the view of the hard-line Afrikaners. Yet, in the early 1900s, the Afrikaners were perhaps the least strong of South Africa's white groups. Already economically weak before their defeat in the Anglo-Boer War, many had lost their farms and businesses in the fighting. Although they outnumbered the British, they formed a new class of poor whites who flocked to the mines and cities in search of work.

The fact that the hard-line Afrikaners emerged to lead the country and shape its policies within fifty years of the war can be traced in part to their strong sense of independence and tradition. They rode to power on the crest of a wave of Afrikaner nationalism—a tide of feeling that was both anti-British and antiblack.

STRUGGLES IN
POLITICS AND LABOR

From the beginning of the Union, the Afrikaners were divided. One group, led by Prime Minister Louis Botha, favored cooperation with the British. In racial policy, these people were for the most part content with the status quo —letting each province of the Union determine its own stand. Botha's wide popularity and moderate stance won him broad support, and he served as prime minister from the founding of the Union to his death in 1919.

A second group of Afrikaners, however, resented the British, who had become the country's business leaders and were on the whole better off than the Afrikaners. With the defeat they had suffered in the war, these people saw the possibility of becoming second-class citizens. And they feared that their position in society would deteriorate even faster if blacks were given rights. Economic rights for blacks might cost them jobs, and political rights for blacks might cost them their voice in the control of the country. Afrikaner politicians of this stamp often spoke of what they called the *Swart Gevaar*, or black menace. In 1912, a group of these Afrikaners led by James Barry Hertzog broke away from Botha's moderate South African Party and formed the Nationalist Party. It was dedicated to bringing the Afrikaners up to par with the English in wealth, status, and power, and to "the supremacy of the European population in a spirit of Christian trusteeship, utterly rejecting every attempt to mix the races."

Two years later, World War I broke out, and Botha led the country into the war on the side of Britain against Germany. But his decision deepened the split in the country; many Afrikaners thought they owed no support to Britain and should remain neutral. Many were also shocked when the government enlisted some thirty thousand blacks as soldiers. The idea of training blacks as soldiers went against the grain for whites who had so recently fought blacks in frontier wars. The government had to suppress an uprising of discontented Afrikaners, but it went on to fight the war and to take an important part in forming the League of Nations afterward. As a result, South Africa gained a League mandate for the control of

South-West Africa, a former German colony that lay on its northwestern border.

An economic depression followed the war, and the splits in the country widened. When Botha died in 1919, he was succeeded as prime minister by another moderate Boer War general, Jan Christiaan Smuts. Smuts at first managed to stay in power by allying his party with an English-speaking group, the Unionist Party. But in the early 1920s, his control was shaken by a series of strikes and riots by white workers that swept through the mines and the new industries that were starting to develop in the cities. In 1922, the army had to be called in to quell labor riots, and 250 people were killed.

Chief among the white workers' complaints were fears of competition from black workers, who vastly outnumbered them. Black workers were already restricted—they could not strike for higher wages, for example. But this (and the fact that black wages were significantly lower than white wages) only made black workers more attractive to white mine owners. It was the mine owners' attempts to bring more blacks into the mines that set off the 1922 strikes.

Meanwhile, like the poor whites, blacks were pouring into the cities in increasing numbers to find work, despite a complicated set of regulations designed to keep them on their reserves. A black who traveled from his reserve might need ten or a dozen different passes and permits: an identification permit, labor registration, traveling pass, permit to seek work, visitor's permit, and so on. Still, the influx to the cities continued. White workers, already pressed by black competition for jobs, now feared they would have to compete for housing as well. To control the black migration and allay these fears, the Smuts government passed the Natives (Urban Areas) Act of 1923, which set up black townships outside the major cities. The land in these townships was owned by the government; blacks could rent homes but not buy them. The point of the law was clear:

Blacks were considered temporary visitors, to be held at arm's length from the white cities.

In 1924, the government adopted a new law that established collective bargaining procedures for unions and management, and it specifically excluded blacks from such negotiations. This, the Urban Areas Act, the system of reserves and passes, and the other restrictions on black workers didn't satisfy white laborers, however. Whites, as one white labor advocate expressed it, wanted guarantees of jobs that paid wages "a European can live on"; blacks, on the other hand, could and should be paid less. Without such guarantees, white workers would be reduced to doing black work at black wages and would be little more than "white kaffirs."

Hertzog's Nationalist Party backed the white laborers' demands, as did an English-speaking party, the Labour Party. In 1924, these two parties formed a coalition that was able to unseat the Unionists, and Hertzog became prime minister. He began to put in place the laws that formed the foundation of apartheid. One of the first laws extended the color bars in mining work, so that all but the lowest positions were reserved for whites. Hertzog also set up a wage board that systematically raised wages for white work—or "civilized" work—while ignoring black workers. This, the government said, was fair because blacks' aims were "restricted to the base requirements of

Although a political moderate, Jan Smuts instituted a number of laws in the 1920s that laid a foundation for apartheid, including the establishment of separate black townships and the barring of black workers from collective bargaining.

the necessities of life as understood among barbarous and undeveloped peoples."

A second law grew out of the system the British had originally set up in Natal. Passed in 1927, it made the government the "supreme chief" of all blacks on the reserves, with wide powers over them. The government could order a member of a tribe or the entire tribe to move to a certain place or to stay where they were. The law also made it a crime to say or do "anything with the intent to promote any feeling of hostility between natives and Europeans"—a vague restriction that was used to squelch any black complaints of unequal treatment.

Hertzog had a far broader plan for white supremacy, however. He wanted to strip all blacks, including those in the Cape Province, of the right to vote, which he called "the fruit of centuries of civilized government." He proposed a plan whereby Cape blacks would be taken off the regular voter rolls and allowed to elect, separately, a total of seven white representatives to Parliament. At first he couldn't muster enough support for his plan. In fact, as South Africa was hit by the worldwide economic depression of the 1930s and people began to blame the government for their troubles, he feared he would lose power altogether.

To stay in control, Hertzog formed a new coalition in 1934, fusing his party with Smuts's more moderate South African Party to create the United Party. The new party controlled 90 percent of the seats in Parliament, and Hertzog's plan for black voters breezed through in 1936. (Ironically, white voting rights were expanded about this time. White women were given the vote in 1930.) Cape blacks were also denied the right to buy land; in short, they were given the same status as blacks in the other provinces. In exchange for the loss of these rights, a bit more land was added to the reserves: Their total area was expanded to 13 percent of the country. Blacks were also permitted to send representatives to a separate Native Representative Council, but this body had no real power.

By the end of 1936, then, three basic foundations of apartheid were in place: Blacks were restricted to certain areas of the country and entered "white" areas only as migrant workers. They were denied political rights. And they were limited to certain types of work. But this was only the start. Some Afrikaners were infuriated that Hertzog had joined forces with the moderates, and they split to form the Purified National Party (later called simply the National Party). It was this group that was to bring apartheid into full flower.

THE RISE OF
AFRIKANER NATIONALISM

The split in the Afrikaner political parties was a symptom of the growing strength of Afrikaner nationalism. For some, support of the Afrikaner language, culture, and traditions (including racism) reached fanatical proportions. Groups such as the Broederbond, a secret organization dedicated to cleansing the Afrikaner community of all British influence, gained members. There was, in fact, a fair amount of pro-German and pro-Nazi sentiment among some Afrikaner groups in the years leading up to World War II. They were attracted by Adolf Hitler's theories of racial purity and white supremacy.

The greatest expression of the growing nationalistic feeling was the Ox Wagon Trek of 1938, a reenactment of the Great Trek of 1835. Afrikaners drove ox wagons along the routes taken by the Voortrekkers, with women dressed in traditional aprons and bonnets and men in the long beards and black jackets their forefathers wore. Relays of runners carried burning torches across the country to Pretoria, where a monument honoring the Voortrekkers was erected. On December 16, the anniversary of the Blood River battle, bonfires lit the hills around Pretoria. One Afrikaner writer described the celebration: "The hill is on fire; on fire with Afrikaner fire. . . . There is hope for your future, South Africa!"

World War II deepened the political split among the Afrikaners. Smuts supported entering the war on Britain's side, and Hertzog opposed it. Smuts won backing in Parliament and so became prime minister once again, with Hertzog resigning. Both English and Afrikaner South Africans then mounted a strong war effort, and the war also helped boost South Africa's growing industries. The war years saw some small gains for blacks, too. The white members of Parliament who represented them took their job seriously, voiced black concerns, and were able to win worker's compensation and pensions for black workers.

But, gradually, the various dissenting Afrikaner groups gathered under the banner of the National Party, led by Daniel F. Malan. Malan was a fanatical racist and Afrikaner nationalist. By playing on resentment of the English and fear of the "black menace," he was able to increase his support. In 1948, in an upset that took everyone by surprise, the National Party won the parliamentary elections, and Malan became prime minister.

The National Party was as surprised as everyone else at its victory, and its leaders did not expect to hold power long unless they took steps to secure their position. They quickly set about redrawing election-district boundaries and even increased the size of Parliament to include five white members from the territory of South-West Africa, where their support was strong. These moves ensured their hold on the government. Meanwhile, Malan began to introduce an elaborate program of legislation designed to make apartheid—an Afrikaans word meaning "separateness"—the law of the land.

APARTHEID

Malan's program differed from earlier laws, which basically legalized segregation and discrimination, in that it was far broader. It envisioned a society where each race lived entirely apart—separate homes, separate jobs, separate churches, separate theaters and restaurants, and so on. There would be no racial mixing of any kind, especially in marriage. Blacks would enter white areas only to sell their services as laborers; then they would return to their own areas. Coloureds and Indians were included in Malan's plan, too. While earlier Afrikaner leaders, including Hertzog, had accepted a degree of coloured-white integration as inevitable, the advocates of apartheid wanted no part of it.

Theologians of the Dutch Reformed Church cited scripture in support of apartheid. Quoting passages from Genesis, Deuteronomy, and Acts, they said that God had first created all men as a single race. At the time of the Tower of Babel, however, He divided them, "scattered them over the face of the whole earth," and set boundaries between them, determining the places where they should live. Apartheid, then, was not simply desirable—it was God's will, and applying it was a religious duty.

Apartheid's supporters also justified this rigid, all-encompassing segregation with a practical theory: It would be in the best interests of all the races if each developed separately, according to its own traditions and in its own area. That could only happen if contact between the races was kept to a minimum. In practice, however, apartheid did far more to halt development for blacks and coloureds than it did to further it.

Three central laws were passed quickly. The first required everyone in the country to be classified in one of three racial groups—white, native (black), or coloured (including Indians and other Asians, who later were classified as a separate group). The goal of this law was to prevent people from "passing" from one racial group to another if their appearance made it possible; all people over sixteen had to carry identification documents showing their race. A second law barred marriage between whites and people of any other race. In 1957, this law was backed up by another one that forbade "immoral acts" between whites and people of other races. On occasion, even a kiss led to criminal charges. The punishment could be as much as seven years in prison.

The third law was the Group Areas Act of 1950, a highly complex piece of legislation that gave the government power to declare which racial group might live where. Throughout South Africa, and especially in the cities, areas were marked out for black, coloured, and white occupation. In many cases, this law forced people to move out of homes they had lived in for years, simply because the area had suddenly been declared "for whites only." Because blacks were already mostly segregated in townships and reserves, coloureds and Indians felt the effects of this law the hardest. From the law's adoption in 1950 until 1984, more than 126,000 families were moved. In one case, an Indian man in Pretoria served three prison terms rather than leave a home he had lived in for thirty-seven years.

Malan and the other National Party leaders also set about ensuring that all political power would be held in white hands. Blacks, it was true, were already on a separate voter roll and were restricted to their seven white representatives; Indians, similarly, were allowed to elect four whites to Parliament. But in Cape Province, coloureds were still able to register along with whites, and the National Party felt threatened by this. In 1951, it pushed legislation through Parliament that would deny coloureds equal voting rights for the first time in the Cape's history. Years later, Hendrik Verwoerd—a National Party politician who was one of the architects of apartheid and who served as prime minister—explained their position this way: "It is a very simple and perfectly clear situation. If we eliminate the Bantu from our political life . . . then the position is that we have a white majority in South Africa and two minority groups [coloured and Indian]. . . . If the minority group becomes the tail that wags the dog because it happens to hold the balance of power between two equally strong parties, a colossal injustice is done towards the majority of the people, because it then means that the minority rules the majority."

The law that disenfranchised coloured voters touched off riots in Cape Town, and South Africa's Supreme Court promptly declared it unconstitutional; it amounted to a change in the constitution, which would require a two-thirds majority in Parliament. In response, the National Party simply increased the size of the Senate until it had enough votes for the majority required. Parliament passed the law in 1956—and also took the step of declaring itself above the rule of any court. Under the new setup, coloureds were allowed five white representatives in Parliament. A powerless coloured representative council, with a third of its members appointed by the government and the rest elected, was also established. By this time, the movement that had opposed the law in 1951 had lost steam, and there was little protest to what seemed an inevitable loss of rights.

Meanwhile, apartheid was also being applied to blacks. Here the idea was to separate blacks from the rest of society altogether: They would be ruled by local chiefs in segregated areas, under white trusteeship. This plan was built on the earlier laws that had set aside reserves and made the government the "supreme chief" of blacks; and, again, there was a theory to justify it. Said one government minister: "The natives of this country do not all belong to the same tribe or race. They have different languages and customs. We are of the opinion that the solidarity of the tribes should be preserved and that they should develop along the lines of their own national character and tradition." It was fitting that this development should take place on the reserves, he added, because "that is where the eventual home of the natives will be, and there they will have to learn to govern themselves." Separating blacks along tribal lines wasn't simply a matter of respect for traditions, however. It also allowed whites to foster divisions among blacks, so that resistance to apartheid was weakened.

Based on this philosophy, the reserves were declared Bantustans, or "homelands," for various tribal groups: Transkei and Ciskei for the Xhosa, KwaZulu for the Zulu,

Lebowa for the North Sotho, Bophuthatswana for the Tswana, and so on. There were ten in all. All the homelands were desperately poor and far too small to contain the black population. For the most part, they weren't even proper geographical units; each was cut up into many sections by white settlements and landholdings, so that they were in fact formed by nearly a hundred tiny black enclaves. The homelands, the government said, were to be self-governing (although the central government would retain control of security, foreign affairs, communications, immigration, and most transportation). The opposite side of that coin, of course, was that blacks would lose even their token representation in the national government. Ultimately, the homelands would become independent— at which point blacks would no longer be citizens of South Africa, and the government would have no responsibility for them.

When this plan was announced in 1951, it sparked revolt in Transkei and several other areas. Chiefs who opposed the plan were deposed and vanished; in some groups, that move set off civil wars. Blacks split on the issue. Some favored separate development as a way of gaining control over their own affairs. Others pointed to the poverty of the homelands and pressed for an integrated, multiracial society instead.

The resistance and turmoil meant that it took the government ten years to implement the plan, but it succeeded in the end. First the black representative council was dissolved, and tribal and regional authorities were set up to govern black affairs. Then, in 1959, blacks lost their representation in Parliament; instead, separate governments were set up in the homelands. These governments had limited power, and any of their actions could be vetoed by the all-white Parliament. Two years later, all Africans living outside the homelands were absorbed into the system—they were assigned to one or another homeland, and told that that was the only place where they could vote or hold any political rights.

Transkei was the first homeland to become self-governing, in 1963. It was also the first to become independent, in 1976, followed by Bophuthatswana, Venda, and Ciskei. But no country other than South Africa grants diplomatic recognition to the homelands or considers them independent states—they remain too closely linked to South Africa. And although all South African blacks are assigned to homelands, only about half actually live in them.

The architects of apartheid recognized that blacks would still come to the mines and black townships near white areas to find jobs; the homelands were too small, and their land too poor, to support the black population. Indeed, without black workers, the South African economy would collapse. The homelands policy simply provided a mechanism through which blacks could be denied political rights and through which those whose labor was not required could be kept out of the way. Meanwhile, other laws extended apartheid into all walks of life.

All blacks living or traveling out of a homeland were required to carry a pass, or reference book, at all times. The pass gave details about their background and showed the necessary permits that allowed them to be away from their homeland. Failure to produce the pass on demand was a criminal offense, and the law resulted in tens of thousands of arrests each year. Many offenders had simply forgotten their passes at home or had misplaced them somewhere. Others were squatters or other unauthorized people, who could then be forceably removed to a homeland. Over the years, this law became one of the heaviest burdens of apartheid.

The National Party also extended color bars to new areas of employment. Blacks were forbidden to do skilled construction work in white areas, for example. In 1956, a new law gave the minister of labor blanket power to apply a color bar to any job, and, over the years, blacks were barred from truck driving, electrical work, clothing manufacture, motor vehicle assembly, and many other trades. In Natal, blacks could not tend bar; in Cape Town, they

This man shows his pass book,
without which no black could travel
in South Africa until the hated
pass laws were changed in 1986.

could not be firemen, ambulance drivers, or traffic police. (In practice, employers found that the color bars worked against them—very often, there simply weren't enough white workers to fill jobs. The law allowed the government to make exceptions to its rulings, and in many areas such exceptions became the rule and blacks began to move into once-forbidden fields.)

Education had been under the control of the provinces when the Union of South Africa was formed. Most primary and secondary schools had always been segregated, and black education was nowhere near the level of white education. No law barred a black who reached university level from attending school, however, and many South African universities admitted blacks. But now a new theory came to the fore—"Bantu education"—custom-tailored for the role blacks would play in society. Under this program, black children were taught separately and in tribal languages; they learned English and Afrikaans in secondary school. Courses emphasized tribal traditions and practical skills. In 1959, the government carried the plan one step further and segregated higher education. Separate colleges were established for coloured, Indian, Xhosa, Zulu, and Sotho-Tswana students. (The National Party also promoted separate schools for English-speaking and Afrikaans-speaking students as a way of keeping the more liberal English influence out of Afrikaner schools.)

Another group of laws established what became known as petty apartheid—social segregation. In many cases, social segregation was already a fact; blacks and whites lived apart and tended to stay apart. But the National Party preferred to make this segregation law. Civic halls, post offices, libraries, parks, theaters, hotels, restaurants, beaches, sports facilities, and other public areas were designated for one racial group or another. Since many of these facilities were already in white areas, whites got the best of them; there was no provision in the laws for equal facilities for the other groups. In some cases, areas were rezoned to put the facilities in white hands.

By the early 1960s, most of the major laws setting up apartheid were in place. Their combined effect was to condemn many blacks to a life of poverty and repression. There wasn't enough good farmland in the homelands to support even those who lived there; many survived on old-age pensions or government welfare. A farmer who wanted to get ahead could not, since in most areas no one was permitted to farm more than one small unit of land. In most families, then, someone would have to leave and find work as a contract laborer outside the homeland. Usually this was the husband, who would spend most of the year living at a hostel in a black township, like those set up under the 1923 Urban Areas Act, or at a mine. Family life was weakened, and children grew up hardly seeing their fathers.

Life might be better if both parents found city jobs and the entire family moved to a township. But, particularly in the early years of apartheid, most townships lacked services like paved roads, electricity, and indoor plumbing. Housing was limited, and conditions were crowded. Township government, by local councils, was weak and ineffective, and crime rates were high. All the same, some blacks managed to found successful businesses or move into skilled trades, and a black middle class began to develop in the townships.

Coloureds and Indians occupied a middle ground between blacks and whites, politically and economically. For them, apartheid blocked hopes and aspirations of achieving true equality with whites. Some, seeing that they were better off than blacks, chose not to complain. Others rightly resented the new laws. They began to increasingly ally themselves with blacks, as members of similar oppressed groups.

For whites, apartheid gave the strength of law to the life of privilege they had established for themselves. The years since the founding of the Union had seen Afrikaner fortunes improve. As the ruling class in Africa's wealthiest country, with strong laws ensuring a ready supply of cheap

Black workers living at the Kimberley Diamond Mine cook their food outdoors in the compound.

labor, they were in a comfortable position. Many families could afford servants. Some whites felt more secure with the laws in place and pointed to the theories behind apartheid to justify their position. Others expressed doubts and misgivings. But as yet, only a few were ready to openly protest against the injustices created by the system.

Apartheid produced bizarre situations—situations that made the country seem like Alice's Wonderland with a dark twist. Government censors banned publications to silence dissent and talk of racial equality; briefly, it's said, they even banned the children's classic *Black Beauty* because of its title. The dissident Afrikaner writer André Brink described other such situations in his essay *After Soweto*: A coloured orchestra plays at a white wedding but is separated from the guests by a net curtain to avoid "racial mixing." A white South African and a Vietnamese woman, married abroad, are jailed for immorality because they belong to different races. An Indian doctor cannot perform surgery on his white patients because the operating theater is for whites only. An ambulance rushes to the scene of an accident but takes only one victim, a white, to the hospital—another victim, black, must wait for a black ambulance.

The only major area of life where apartheid was not established by law was religion. The government attempted to segregate churches in 1957, but the outcry was so great that it backed down. Not all religious groups were opposed to apartheid. The Dutch Reformed Church and the Presbyterian Church were organized into black and white units, with separate congregations. But the Anglican, Roman Catholic, Methodist, and other churches rejected apartheid and condemned it as un-Christian.

In fact, these churches formed part of a simmering opposition that slowly grew as the government tightened the screws of apartheid. The opposition included whites as well as blacks and coloureds, and it came from outside the country as well as from within it.

6

RESISTANCE

More than any other, the picture people outside South Africa hold of the country today is one of protest—often violent protest. Despite government attempts to block news reports, the images of blacks singing and chanting as they march down the streets, of black demonstrators battling armed police, have been shown around the world.

Such protests aren't a new development. White supremacy didn't emerge in South Africa without resistance from blacks and other nonwhite groups; resistance was there from the beginning. And as the effects of apartheid became stronger and more widely felt, protest grew as well. At times—and today is one such time—the resistance has brought the country to the brink of civil war.

FROM GANDHI
TO SHARPEVILLE

Once whites gained control of the land, most nonwhite protests were small and largely ineffective. Most blacks and coloureds accepted the fact that the whites were in control; the white man was the *baas*, or boss, and there was little that could be done about it. But around the turn of the century, some groups began to take action.

One of the earliest organized protests came from the Indians of Natal. It was begun by Mohandas K. Gandhi, who was later to lead India to independence. Gandhi had studied law in Britain and came to South Africa in 1893, planning to practice his profession for a year. Almost immediately, he encountered the growing discrimination faced by all Natal Indians at that time. He ended up staying in the country for twenty-one years, organizing marches and strikes that, often as not, ended with his imprisonment. South Africa, in fact, became the proving ground for the techniques of nonviolent protest he later used in India.

Before he returned home in 1915, Gandhi won the repeal of the head tax all Indians were required to pay and a promise from the Smuts government for just treatment for his people. But the promise was short-lived— within five years, new laws limited the Indians' rights to own land and run businesses. An Indian rights group, the South African Indian Congress, continued to protest. But as apartheid began to take effect, the Indians found themselves on the wrong side of the color bars in housing and employment.

Meanwhile, however, Gandhi's protests had served as a model for other groups. When the Union was formed denying the vote to all blacks but those in the Cape, and when legislation passed in the first few years limited blacks' rights to own land and work at skilled jobs, blacks formed the group that would become the African National Congress (ANC). At first, this group was small and quite conservative. Its members were mostly blacks who had been educated abroad or at missions, and they exerted quiet pressure on whites, asking for better treatment for their people and for greater political rights. But the wind was blowing the other way. As the hard-line Afrikaners gained power, blacks lost ground.

The changes brought by the two world wars—the growth of industry and the thousands of blacks who moved to the cities to find work—also changed the character of black resistance. Younger, more militant blacks began to join the ANC, and they were impatient with the moderate stance the organization had taken. In 1944, they formed the ANC Youth League, for blacks aged twelve through forty. One of the group's founders was Anton Muziwakhe Lembede, who (unlike the early ANC leaders but like many of the young members) was the self-educated son of a laborer. In several tense confrontations, Lembede and the Youth League pressed the ANC to take action—demonstrations, strikes, civil disobedience. And within a few years, the older group had begun to agree.

The National Party's ascent to power in 1948 was one of the main forces behind this switch to stronger black protest. As the party began to put apartheid in place in 1949 and 1950, demonstrations grew, and some riots broke out. The ANC issued its most militant statement yet, rejecting the white government and all forms of segregation. It also elected new leaders. Lembede had died in 1947, but three Youth Leaguers were named to the ANC's executive board. All three were to become powerful forces in the black movement over the next few years.

The first was Nelson Mandela, a tall man with a commanding personality who had been born into a chief's family in Transkei. Mandela had been a founding member of the Youth League and had been expelled from one university for leading student protests. He had later studied law at another school in Johannesburg. The second, Oliver Tambo, had shared many of the same experiences. He, too, was born in Transkei, had studied law and been expelled for taking part in a student strike, and had joined the Youth League at its start. A quiet and thoughtful man, he taught at a top black school in Johannesburg, where his views influenced many of the students. Walter Sisulu, the last of the three, had a different background. His family were Transkei peasants, and he had worked as a laborer in the mines and in several cities. A short, stocky, bespectacled figure, he had organized several labor strikes.

In 1952, the ANC launched the Defiance Campaign, a series of demonstrations and protests using Gandhi's passive resistance techniques. The government's response was to crack down, hard. From June to December of 1952, more than eight thousand blacks were arrested, and more than fifty black leaders were banned—that is, forbidden to attend gatherings, write or speak for publication, hold any office, or travel in specified areas. The banning was made possible by a law, adopted in 1950, that was allegedly designed to suppress Communism. It defined Communism in such broad terms that virtually all protest fell under it. Some of the black protestors were, in fact, leftist in their politics, as were some whites of the day. South Africa's Communist Party had formed in the 1920s and had been one of the few white groups to recognize the blacks' demands, and many blacks were drawn to it even after it was banned. Most of the protestors, however, simply opposed apartheid and wanted equal rights.

In 1953, new laws, giving the government even broader powers to deal with protestors, were put into place. One imposed stiff penalties—whipping, fines, confiscation of property, imprisonment—for passive resistance. Another allowed the government to declare a "state of emergency" and rule by decree, without consulting Parliament, whenever it saw fit. Under a state of emergency, free speech could be restricted, meetings forbidden, curfews imposed, and people arrested on the mere suspicion that they planned to demonstrate.

Meanwhile, the National Party continued with its apartheid program. When the government began to issue passes to blacks and to forceably remove those who lived "illegally" in the cities, the resistance turned violent. Blacks openly burned their passes and rioted, and there

*Walter Sisulu, seated on the truck at far right,
was General Secretary of the African National
Congress when he was arrested during
the Defiance Campaign in 1952.*

were more arrests and bannings. The ANC called on other rights groups for cooperation and support: the South African Indian Congress; the South African Coloured People's Organization; trade unions that opposed the government's steps to deny blacks collective bargaining rights; and the South African Congress of Democrats, a white group that included many leftists and opposed the government's policies.

These groups banded together to form the Congress Alliance. In 1954, they sent three thousand delegates to a mixed-race antiapartheid conference near Kliptown, a coloured township outside Johannesburg. Meeting for two days in an open field, the delegates adopted the Freedom Charter, a document that promoted equal rights for all. On the second day, however, armed police took over the speakers' platform, wrote down the names and addresses of everyone present, and broke up the meeting.

The government then tightened its surveillance of all the groups. In 1956, it arrested 156 blacks (mostly from the ANC) and whites, accusing them of a Communist plot to overthrow the government. The government spent the next five years vainly trying to prove its charges in court, in proceedings that became known as the Treason Trials. While most of the defendants were eventually let go, the trials sapped their strength, ruined many financially, and deprived the opposition of many of its best leaders at a critical time.

Although some whites supported the Congress Alliance, most reacted to the nonwhite protests with fear. They were thankful that the government dealt harshly with protestors. The Labour Party was the only legal white political group to campaign openly against apartheid, and it failed to win a single seat in Parliament in the 1958 elections. But repression could not smother the protests. ANC president Albert John Luthuli, who was awarded the 1960 Nobel Peace Prize, said, "We shall never rest content until the domestic principle which is conceded for Europeans is extended to include the entire population. . . . Our aim is neither white supremacy nor black supremacy but a common South African multi-racial society, based upon friendship, equality of rights, and mutual respect."

In a sense, the whites' suppression of black protest helped realize their own worst fears. The harder they tried to hold a lid on protest, the greater the pressure of the resistance became. Frustrated with their lack of progress, a group of blacks split off from the ANC in 1960 to form the Pan-African Congress (PAC). Its goal was not a multi-racial society but a black society—"Africa for the Africans" —structured along vaguely socialist lines. On March 21, 1960, the PAC organized a peaceful protest: Blacks were to present themselves at police stations around the country without their passes, to show their defiance of apartheid. Large crowds gathered outside police stations in many towns and, in most cases, were peacefully dispersed. But in Sharpeville, in the Transvaal, the event took a tragic turn. Police opened fire on the crowd, killing 69 people and wounding 178.

Sharpeville brought South Africa to a new stage in which the struggle between black and white was increasingly marked by terrorism on the one hand and brute force on the other. South Africa was not the only country where racial protests sparked violence. At the same time that the South African protests were growing, civil rights demonstrators in the United States were being arrested and often beaten. But there were major differences between the two situations. For one, mistreatment of the U.S. demonstrators outraged whites and blacks alike; ultimately, it led to concrete gains for blacks. This did not happen in South Africa. There, whites were (and are) a minority; black rights, they feared, would mean a loss of power for them. Verwoerd, who was prime minister at the time of Sharpeville, stated the white position: "We must let the world know we are fighting for our existence. If we waver we will lose everything."

But the plight of blacks in South Africa did not go unnoticed around the world. The government found itself facing increasing criticism and pressure abroad, especially from fellow members of the Commonwealth, to change its policies. Its reply reflected both the whites' belief that they were fighting for their lives and the tradition of Afrikaner independence. With a referendum showing that 52.5 percent of whites approved the action, South Africa withdrew from the Commonwealth and reformed itself as a republic in May 1961. In a sense, the Afrikaners had circled their wagons, or formed a *laager*, much as they had when under attack in frontier days.

RESISTANCE
GOES UNDERGROUND

The Sharpeville incident was followed by a state of emergency that lasted until the end of August. More than eighteen thousand people, most of them black, were arrested and held without trial during this period. The ANC and the PAC were declared illegal organizations, and many black leaders fled the country or went into hiding.

Black resistance was forced underground. Both the ANC and the PAC established military branches and began to train members as guerrilla fighters in secret bases. They managed to pull off some successful acts of sabotage in the early 1960s, blowing up power stations, post offices, and railway junctions and cutting telephone lines. In March 1961, representatives of black groups met and agreed to set aside their differences to work against apartheid; they appointed a national council and chose Nelson Mandela, who succeeded Luthuli as ANC leader, to head it. The government promptly ordered his arrest, but he escaped.

White support for apartheid, meanwhile, solidified. In elections in 1961, the National Party won 105 seats, and the United Party 50. Even the United Party politicians supported white supremacy. The Progressive Party, a new group that had split off from the United Party, was the only party that opposed it and managed to gather enough votes to send a single representative to Parliament (Helen Suzman, who remained her party's sole representative until 1975). With that clear mandate, the government set about increasing its powers to deal with unrest. Sabotage was ruled a form of treason; even receiving training in guerrilla methods was punishable by sentences that ranged from five years' imprisonment to death. Censorship was imposed on the press. The police were virtually freed from any restraint and allowed to detain anyone without a warrant for ninety days.

The police lost no time in using their new powers, and arrests and bannings increased. At first violence increased, too. There were riots near Cape Town late in 1962; early in 1963, five whites were killed in Transkei; a number of progovernment black chiefs were assassinated. But by making sweeping arrests, the police managed to crush the unrest. Prisoners detained under the new laws had no right to visitors or legal counsel. They were held in isolation and allowed outside for exercise once a day, for an hour or less. Many people who were detained said they were treated harshly and tortured, with beatings and electric shocks.

In mid-1963, the police surprised eight Congress Alliance leaders at their secret headquarters outside Johannesburg. The captured included Nelson Mandela, Walter Sisulu, and four other blacks; Ahmed Kathrada, an Indian; and Denis Goldberg, a white. Evidence, including a cache of explosives, linked them to sabotage. They didn't deny the charge. Mandela, in fact, made an eloquent speech defending the use of force: "Government violence can do only one thing and that is to breed counter-violence . . . if there is no dawning of sanity on the part of the government, the dispute between the government and my people will finish up by being settled in violence." All were sentenced to life imprisonment. During this same period, at least two thousand others were brought to court in mass

Nelson Mandela, a leader of the
African National Congress,
is shown here around the
time of his arrest in 1963.

political trials and charged with sabotage and other violations of the new laws.

The crackdown effectively suppressed black resistance for the rest of the 1960s. A network of police spies in black areas made it unwise to even talk about political matters. The white government had successfully denied blacks any legal means of dissent, and it appeared to have crushed illegal dissent with equal success. Edgar Brookes, a white who had been elected to the Senate by blacks and who supported their cause, wrote, "[It is] nauseating to hear those who have reduced Africans to silence . . . boasting of that silence as a proof of happiness and contentment."

National Party strength continued to grow in Parliament, and in the late 1960s the party took final steps to cement its power: It segregated all political parties, and it abolished the token representation that Cape coloureds had held in the legislature.

THE TRADE UNIONS

Besides political dissent, there was another side to black protest—the labor unions. Black unions had been vigorously suppressed by the government, but that did not stop blacks from forming their own, unregistered unions and staging illegal strikes to demand better wages and working conditions.

From the 1920s on, black workers' groups figured more and more as a force in South African industry. By 1945, an umbrella group called the Council of Non-European Trade Unions had some 158,000 members, many of them mine workers. A massive mine workers' strike in 1946 closed twelve mines and slowed production at many more. But such strikes produced few results for the workers because both government and employers refused to recognize black unions as legitimate worker representatives. The National Party government began to take steps against the unions soon after it came to power, jailing or banning union leaders and organizers. In the 1950s, the number of blacks in labor unions dropped to about 20,000, where it stayed throughout the 1960s.

The labor movement came to life again in 1973–74, when workers around Durban staged a series of strikes against industry. The strikes spread to other cities, and in all an estimated seventy-five thousand workers walked off their jobs. These actions were mostly organized by the workers in each factory or industry, rather than by any national labor or political group. The strikers were mainly concerned with wages and working conditions, rather than political demands, and they won some concessions. Nevertheless, the government stepped in and made sure that the strike leaders would take no further role, so that the labor movement would not grow. But the Durban strikes had demonstrated one thing clearly: Black workers had power, and they could use it through strikes.

CRACKS IN
THE FOUNDATION

At the very moment that the reign of white supremacy seemed absolute, cracks began to appear in the foundation of apartheid. The government showed that it was not immune to world criticism when, in the late 1960s, it allowed a nonwhite to play on a visiting rugby team. To some Afrikaners, this was heresy; to others, it was long overdue.

Increasingly, after Sharpeville and the repressive measures that followed, whites began to question the morality of apartheid. Even in the Dutch Reformed Church, which had long cited Scripture to prove that racial segregation was God's will, there were doubters. Beyers Naude, a minister whose father had helped found the secret white organization called the Broederbond, was one of the first to turn against apartheid. By the late 1960s, he had been joined by others.

The numbers of whites who opposed apartheid were

still small. But other forces were eroding the government's plan. More Afrikaners were leaving their farms and moving to the cities to work in business and industry, the fields traditionally dominated by the English-speaking whites. They soon discovered the value of a free labor market, in which employers would be free to hire whomever they wished. Industrial color bars began to be widely discarded by the 1970s.

At the same time, a new movement called Black Consciousness was forming among blacks. Like the earlier and now banned PAC, it stressed pride and independence for its people—in much the same way that various "black power" movements did for U.S. blacks at this time. The South African Students' Organization (SASO), formed by black students in 1968, was a major advocate of this view. SASO's founder, and the major figure in the Black Consciousness movement, was Steve Biko, a compelling and highly intelligent leader. Biko had lost patience with white authorities in the mid-1960s when his brother was arrested on suspicion of terrorism and he himself was interrogated about his brother's activities and then expelled from school. He later attended a nonwhite medical school in Natal.

SASO called for better education and job opportunities. But Black Consciousness was less an organized political movement than a philosophical one—Biko and its other leaders stressed that blacks would have to be confident of their power to win their rights. "Black man, you're on your own," was the movement's catchphrase, and it drew its strength from young urban blacks and from Indians and coloureds as well. SASO attracted the attention of the authorities, but because it did not advocate violence it was not immediately banned. And it swept the schools and universities.

The ideas behind Black Consciousness played a part in the Soweto uprising of 1976, one of the worst clashes yet between blacks and the government. But the immediate cause of the uprising was education. Under the Bantu edu-

Although the wall of apartheid was beginning to crack in 1970 when this photograph was taken, the man pictured would still have been subjected to a fine of about $20, or 20 days in prison, if caught sitting on a bench reserved for whites.

cation system that the government had set up, black children were being taught in classes of fifty or sixty, with poorly qualified teachers, little equipment, and rudimentary classrooms. The government paid so little for black education that parents had to pay a supplement to keep their children in school (white education, in contrast, was paid entirely by government funds). And in 1976, the government announced that henceforth, instruction in black schools would be given in Afrikaans. Black students were stunned. Up to now, Afrikaans had been taught as a second language in high school, and most of them had a weak grasp of it. Many saw the change as part of a government plan to put learning even further out of their reach.

In Soweto, black students organized a protest. On June 16, several thousand students, mostly in their teens, marched toward a stadium in the northwest part of the township where they planned to hold a rally. Near the stadium, police blocked the march and opened fire, killing two students and throwing the rest into panic. The event touched off months of violence that spread throughout the country. Between 570 and 1,000 people were killed, hundreds more were arrested, and hundreds of other blacks fled the country to guerrilla camps across the border. The requirement for Afrikaans in black schools was dropped, although black education was not improved. But for blacks, the Soweto uprising became a symbol. June 16, as one of the student protestors later told *The New York Times,* "was the date the state confronted us and made us realize we are not protected by the law. It was a date that made us realize we have to have a say in running our country. It forced the majority of blacks to say it hurts when it hurts."

The Black Consciousness movement was one of the casualties of the Soweto uprising. Half a dozen organizations that had formed under its banner were banned, and many of its advocates fled. Biko was arrested. On September 12, 1977, he died in detention—the victim, police said, of "head injuries" sustained in a struggle with his guards. International outcry was so great that the South African government investigated the incident. Although the investigation cleared the guards of wrongdoing, testimony showed that he had been kept in iron chains, made to lie in filth, and, injured and semiconscious, driven 700 miles (1,120 km) in a jolting Land Rover.

Many whites had been taken by surprise by the violence that followed Soweto; they lived such insulated lives that it was easy to assume that all was well among the blacks. Now incidents such as Biko's death increased divisions among them. It became harder and harder to justify apartheid. The Progressive Party (renamed the Progressive Federal Party, or PFP) began to make small gains in elections.

Churches took a leading role in speaking out against the government. The split in the Dutch Reformed Church deepened, so that it no longer supported apartheid universally. Many church leaders also became leaders in the struggle for nonwhite rights. Beyers Naude took a leading position in the South African Council of Churches, an interdenominational group that opposed apartheid. Allan Boesak, a mixed-race Reformed Church leader, helped found the United Democratic Front—a collection of about six hundred local groups that, like the banned ANC, advocated a socialist multiracial state. Desmond Tutu, who became the first black Anglican dean of Johannesburg in 1975, became head of the South African Council of Churches in the late 1970s and spearheaded a campaign of nonviolent protest. He was later elevated to bishop and then archbishop, and in 1984 he became the second antiapartheid activist to be awarded the Nobel Peace Prize.

Within South Africa, church leaders spoke out from pulpits. With most public gatherings banned, church services and funerals became vehicles for protest. Thousands would gather for outdoor services, singing political songs and hearing antiapartheid speeches. As a result, church leaders were often harassed or arrested by the government.

Abroad, the churches played a major role in focusing world attention on South Africa. They called for economic pressures—for countries to halt trade with South Africa and for foreign companies and groups to disinvest, or sell off their South African assets—as well as diplomatic and political pressures. International antiapartheid campaigns produced results, particularly after the Soweto uprising. The United Nations passed resolutions condemning apartheid; South Africa was barred from international sports competitions; a few countries limited trade; and some groups and individuals sold their holdings in companies that did business in South Africa. An international arms embargo made it more difficult for the government to purchase arms abroad.

THE APPEARANCE OF CHANGE

When Pieter Willem Botha became prime minister in 1978, he sensed the shift in the political climate of the country. The government reassessed its stand and determined that it should do away with those aspects of apartheid that were visible and inflammatory—such as the petty apartheid regulations governing social segregation—while keeping the underlying base of geographical and political segregation in place. In this way it hoped to still black unrest and world criticism, while bridging the growing gap between conservatives who favored apartheid and those whites who were beginning to oppose it. Whites, Botha said, must "adapt or die."

In 1979–80, South Africa was hit with a new wave of labor strikes—strikes that, this time, drew greater support than ever from the black community. The strikers demanded recognition of their right to organize as well as better wages, and consumer boycotts backed up their demands. The government could not help but realize that black workers were a growing force—and that that force might be better dealt with if it were brought into the structure of society. One of Botha's first steps, therefore, was to legalize black trade unions. Gradually, new black unions formed and began to attract members.

Then, in 1984, the government took what it felt was a huge step toward accommodating nonwhites. It proposed a new constitution under which the legislature would be divided into three houses: one for whites, one for coloureds, and one for Indians. At the head of the government would be a strong president, chosen by an electoral college made up of those three racial groups.

The constitution was adopted, but in fact it pleased few people and outraged many. Whites still dominated the government, both in the legislature and the electoral college. And the new constitution made no allowance for the overwhelming majority of the people—the blacks. Coloureds and Indians recognized the injustice and showed their displeasure by boycotting elections for the new legislature. In Cape Province, the coloured turnout was roughly 5 percent.

The government made other changes, too. It repealed the ban on interracial marriage, allowed blacks into white universities, removed many minor restrictions, and proposed a plan whereby blacks would be allowed to buy land in specified areas outside the homelands. Courts ruled that before nonwhites could be turned out of their homes to comply with apartheid regulations, alternate housing had

President P. W. Botha has made some changes in South Africa since he became head of the government in 1978, but he has been unwilling to take the necessary steps for establishing equality for all South Africans.

to be available. And in mid-1986, the government replaced the hated black passes with an identity document that would be carried by all races. But these changes merely produced what Desmond Tutu called "the appearance of change"; political power was still strongly in white hands, and blacks were still forced to live in restricted areas. Nonwhites and liberal whites—who by this time made up about 20 percent of the white population—condemned the government for not going far enough. Said Beyers Naude, "Power-sharing, as the government understands it, means not upsetting the apple cart of Afrikaner political dominance."

The cosmetic changes were enough to anger conservative whites, however. Two groups, the Conservative Party and the smaller Herstigte Nationale Party, gained strength as hard-line Afrikaners became disillusioned with the National Party's new course. The Afrikaner Resistance Movement, an extremist group, vowed to fight to maintain white supremacy. These groups made up another 20 percent of whites, and the government found itself caught between them and the liberals.

At the same time, blacks in growing numbers were becoming increasingly impatient for true change. Individual labor unions merged into federations that, more and more, became political spokesmen for blacks. In 1985 the largest of these federations, the Congress of South African Trade Unions (COSATU) was formed, linking thirty-three unions with a combined membership of five hundred thousand.

The unions joined other black organizations that managed to remain legal by not supporting violence. Largest of these was the United Democratic Front, which many people said was basically a stand-in for the exiled ANC. Inkatha, a movement headed by the Zulu leader Mangosuthu Gatsha Buthelezi, drew support from some one million blacks, mainly among the Zulu. Its goal, too, was a multiracial state. The Azanian People's Organization became the heir to the "Africa for the Africans" philosophies of the PAC and the Black Consciousness movement. ("Azania" is the term blacks of this organization prefer in place of "South Africa.")

But the illegal groups—the PAC and the ANC—continued to draw support. Of the two, the ANC was by far the stronger. The ANC's Nelson Mandela was believed by many to be the most widely respected leader among South African blacks. With Mandela in jail, Oliver Tambo led the group from headquarters in Lusaka, Zambia, lobbying for world support while sponsoring guerrilla attacks within South Africa. The ANC fighters were based in countries bordering South Africa. Arms and explosives were supplied chiefly by the Soviet Union, although the ANC was also backed by many Western antiapartheid groups.

Thus the partial reforms of the South African government did little to satisfy any of the country's deeply opposed groups. Young blacks in the townships, meanwhile, became more and more embittered. Increasingly, they dreamed of becoming guerrilla fighters who would take their people's battle for equal rights into the streets.

7

SOUTH AFRICA TODAY

The question most important to South Africa today is whether the country can avoid a bloody civil war. The end of the immorality act and of most aspects of petty apartheid has done away with some of the daily pain for nonwhites. But as yet the government shows no sign of permitting true equality for people of all races or anything but limited power sharing with blacks. And as it tries to satisfy both liberals and conservatives, its reforms are matched, tit for tat, with increased repression.

After the country's new constitution was adopted in 1984, ignoring black rights, black resistance and anger heated to the boiling point. Riots broke out in a number of townships. The government answered with two states of emergency: a limited one affecting black areas in 1985 and a more sweeping, countrywide declaration in 1986. Some two thousand people died in violence in the two-year period, and many thousands more were detained. Thus South Africa, with all its resources and extraordinary potential, remains poised on the brink of disaster.

LIVING WITH TENSION

For people of all races, the mood in the country has become one of tension. Most of the violence has been confined to black areas and hasn't affected whites directly. Many whites, then, have gone on with life as usual—working, shopping, getting together for backyard barbecues on weekends. But the U.S. writer and social scientist Vincent Crapanzano, who studied South African whites, found that underlying this appearance of normal life was a mood of waiting— "waiting for something, anything to happen." Meanwhile, because the black population is increasing at a faster rate, whites are increasingly outnumbered. Blacks now outnumber whites by five to one. By the year 2000, the ratio is expected to be nine to one.

Some whites have left the country, either because they could no longer justify their government's actions or because they saw an inevitable end to their privileged way of life. In the mid-1980s, South Africa's white population began to drop for the first time in its history. Real estate values in some of the pleasant white suburbs have fallen sharply. But most whites are unwilling to leave; South Africa is the place where they have built their homes and businesses and where their families have lived for generations. "I belong in Africa," one white woman told a *New York Times* reporter. "My son was born here. We're all fighting for our rights. The whites are fighting for their rights just as the blacks are."

Of the 4.5 million whites who remain, Afrikaners make up about 60 percent, and English-speakers, 40 percent. Afrikaners, many of them firm supporters of apartheid, continue to dominate the government. But many of the old social distinctions between the two groups are disappearing. The Afrikaners are no longer mostly farmers, while the English-speakers no longer control business and industry to the extent they once did. Instead, many in both groups enjoy a middle-class, suburban life-style that Americans might recognize.

Likewise, people in both groups recognize that some form of black power sharing is unavoidable, and many agree that the government's reforms are too little and too slow. But they are unsure what form power sharing should take. They look uneasily to the north, to countries such as Mozambique and Angola, where white fortunes have not fared well under black majority rule. And political divisions have heightened, with extremist groups like the Afrikaner Resistance Movement balanced by other groups such as Black Sash, a white organization that works to help blacks caught in the legal tangles that apartheid can create. Whites, as well as blacks, have been arrested for their opposition to apartheid.

Coloureds and Indians find themselves in roughly the position that U.S. blacks held before the civil rights gains of the 1960s: racial minorities discriminated against by law. In many cities, mixed-race areas have been emptied of people, and thousands have been moved out to new housing developments on the fringe of town. The government presents this as an improvement because some of the old neighborhoods were slums, and housing in the new areas is more modern if not deluxe. But to many coloureds, the change is painful; not only have they lost homes and businesses their families may have held for years, but they are now also held at arm's length from the hearts of the cities. In Cape Town the old coloured area, District 6, is a wasteland of weed-filled empty lots near the center of the city.

Some coloureds have made gains in skilled trades and enjoy a middle-class life, and a few of these have begun to reverse the trend to segregation. In large cities like Johannesburg, coloureds and even some blacks have quietly moved into areas that are by law reserved for whites. But many more coloureds have grown bitter over the government's policies. Their political power is still limited under the new constitution. Young coloureds, especially, prefer to be called blacks to show their solidarity in oppression.

Circumstances for the coloureds are still far better than those for most blacks. Blacks have made gains: Education is beginning to improve, and black incomes are rising faster than those of any other group. Booming industry has opened up job opportunities that never existed for their parents. For all their difficulties, South African blacks by some estimates enjoy a better standard of living than that in many of the less affluent countries of Africa. But these gains are relative—they still fall far short of providing a decent life for many blacks. Blacks have no political power whatsoever. Their opportunities are severely limited. In the homelands and the cities, poverty is the rule and malnutrition is commonplace.

The black townships that stand like shadows behind every major South African city are crowded; by one estimate, in mid-1986, as many as eighty thousand people were on waiting lists for housing in Soweto. Such housing ranges from a "three by three"—a shack 3 yards (2.7 m) square— to a typical four-room "matchbox" house. Some families have done better, and there are areas in Soweto where the homes have two stories and attractive yards. These families are the fortunate few, made up of professional and skilled workers and, in some cases, workers for foreign firms that have gone out of their way to improve their workers' lives. But because opportunities for blacks in skilled trades and the professions are still restricted, a good house is the exception. Elsewhere in the township, ten or more people may live in a four-room home. Many areas in the townships are still without electricity and paved roads, and the plumbing is outdoors. Wages are so low that, despite these conditions, rent and utilities take up a significant portion of the average black worker's pay.

Conditions are even worse in the shantytowns, where blacks who cannot find room in the townships live illegally and face the threat of eviction daily. Some homes are tin shacks; others are constructed out of cardboard or plastic bags so that they can be quickly dismantled should the police appear. Joseph Lelyveld, in his book *Move Your Shadow*, describes the eerie look of one such settlement at night, when cooking fires inside the garbage-bag huts "illuminated these flimsy shelters like Chinese lanterns, with long shadows flickering on their inflammable plastic surfaces."

At least the families inside the plastic tents are together —many people in the townships are forceably separated from their families by the migrant worker system. When a husband works in the city and his wife must stay in a homeland, it's not uncommon for the couple to spend no more than a month or two together in ten years of marriage. Crowding in the townships and protests over family separation have led the government to set up what it calls "closer settlements" in some homelands. Here families can live together while the breadwinners commute to their industrial jobs. Families pay a price for this togetherness. Often the commute is a jolting bus ride of 100 miles (160 km) each way, and the commuters must rise before dawn and return home long after dark. And like the townships closer to the cities, these new settlements are crowded —mile after mile packed solid with tin-roofed huts.

In recent years, turmoil has added to poverty in the townships and shantytowns, so that it is hard to talk about a "normal" life for blacks. Police raid homes where they think radicals or blacks without permits may be living and arrest blacks attending funerals and church services. They have shot and killed children who they said threw stones at their vehicles. Spies and informers within black areas are still the government's chief way of maintaining control, and the threat of arrest, indefinite detention, and torture is present daily. But as violence has increased, black areas have become more and more ungovernable.

Police raids, shootings, and random detentions, terrifying as they are, are only one aspect of violence. Much of the fighting in 1985 and 1986 was among blacks themselves. Local affairs in the townships are supposed to be handled by black councils appointed by the government. In fact, most appointees either resign quickly or face the threat of assassination by radical blacks who see them as stand-ins for white authority. The "comrades," as the radical fighters style themselves, are in turn preyed upon by black vigilante groups who often have the tacit support of the police. In a week-long wave of such fighting that swept through the shantytown of Crossroads, near Cape Town, in 1986, thirty blacks died and as many as thirty thousand were made homeless. The government subsequently bulldozed vast swaths of the shantytown, effectively clearing out the illegal settlers.

Local divisions among blacks are reflected in divisions among the major black political groups. Tribal chiefs in the homelands, as well as the black councils in the townships, enjoy less and less support; many blacks consider them to be stooges of the white government. Beyond that, the ANC and the Inkatha movement disagree: Inkatha rejects the ANC's violent methods and claims the rival group is controlled by Communists, while the ANC says that Inkatha is too willing to compromise with whites. Another difference between these two groups is a tribal one—most Inkatha members are Zulu, while the ANC's leadership and its strength have traditionally come mainly from the Xhosa, Sotha, and Tswana. In fact, violence and acts of sabotage have been heaviest in the eastern Cape, traditionally a Xhosa area. The government is fond of pointing to such divisions as proof that blacks are separate groups, not a single majority, and that they are incapable of governing themselves.

Despite their divisions, however, the black groups have many goals in common. Buthelezi, the Inkatha leader, agrees with the ANC that the release of political prisoners —including Nelson Mandela—must come before any serious discussion of reform with the government. Leaders

In 1986, tension erupted into violence in Crossroads,
a shanty town outside Cape Town.

such as Archbishop Desmond Tutu command respect that crosses tribal and organizational lines. In several cases the wives of jailed leaders have emerged as prominent activists: Albertina Sisulu, wife of Walter Sisulu, is copresident of the United Democratic Front; Winnie Mandela, wife of Nelson Mandela, has drawn support from people in many countries to the struggle against apartheid. Both women have been jailed themselves, and Winnie Mandela was banned for twenty-four years, until 1986. For most of that time, she was forced to live in a sort of internal exile in a black township some 200 miles (320 km) from her home in Soweto. She was restricted from speaking out on political issues, could not be quoted in the press, and could not meet with groups of people other than her immediate family.

UNREST CONTINUES

The 1986 state of emergency was called on the eve of the tenth anniversary of the Soweto uprising, which many black groups planned to observe with strikes, demonstrations, and rallies. The government said that it had evidence that widespread sabotage was planned, and it made wholesale arrests among every group that might be a possible source of dissent—even detaining entire church congregations. Leaders of the United Democratic Front and black trade unions headed the list of the more than eight thousand five hundred arrested in the first weeks of the emergency. Tight new restrictions on the press made it illegal to report news of the turmoil, even the names of people detained.

South African troops, meanwhile, attacked cities in Zambia, Zimbabwe, and Botswana where the government said ANC guerrillas were training. The government also used the opportunity to pass new security laws that would remain in effect after the state of emergency ended. Under these laws, police would be allowed to detain people for

*Archbishop Desmond Tutu and Winnie Mandela,
shown here at a funeral in 1986, have
led the fight against apartheid in South Africa.*

up to six months without trial and to exercise unrestricted power in any area the government said was the site of unrest. President Botha said that capitulation to black demands would be "national suicide."

Thus the government continues to waver between reform and repression, matching talk of improvements for nonwhites with harsh actions. So far, it has been unable to stop nonviolent protests such as strikes, rent strikes, school boycotts, and boycotts of white businesses. But as blacks become increasingly angry and frustrated, violence is increasing. Sabotage has begun to spill over into white areas, as guerrillas have changed their focus from military targets and begun to set bombs in shops and restaurants. The ANC's Oliver Tambo told *Newsweek* magazine in 1985, "I have never thought a bloodbath was not inevitable. I fear that it is not only coming but already here. . . . From now on, whether civilians are likely to die will not be a consideration. We have held off in the past, but it has done nothing to save our people's lives."

To many, then, South Africa seems to be on a downward spiral toward civil war.

SOUTH AFRICA
AND THE WORLD

The events of 1985 and 1986 caused people around the world to condemn the South African government more strongly than ever before. Churches and student organizations led demonstrations against apartheid; celebrities and government officials joined in. Despite the South African government's attempt to keep news of unrest from getting out, the news media gave increasing attention to it. More than a dozen nations, including the United States, recalled their ambassadors to protest the government's actions.

Meanwhile, there was more pressure on foreign companies that do business in South Africa. Opponents of apartheid urged people to divest—to sell any stock they held in these companies, to force them to end their South African operations. By mid-1986, nineteen U.S. states and dozens of cities had voted not to invest their pension funds in companies doing business in South Africa, and many universities and private groups had done the same. Fifty-five international corporations had sold their South African assets (disinvested) and gotten out, although hundreds remained.

Many nations also imposed fresh economic sanctions of one degree or another. The European Economic Community (EEC), which includes most of the Western European nations, banned all new investment in South Africa, as well as imports of South African iron, steel, and gold coins. The Commonwealth of Nations, made up of former British colonies, proposed more sweeping sanctions—including bans on government contracts with South African companies and an end to air links with the country. But Britain, South Africa's major trading partner, was reluctant to go along with these measures. And the United States at first took only limited steps.

The United States had been slow to take a stand against apartheid. Even in the last century, when other Western countries were colonizing Africa, it pursued a hands-off policy. The United States voiced support for Britain in the Anglo-Boer war, and American engineers helped develop South African goldfields. But to most Americans, events in South Africa were of little importance. After World War II, as apartheid developed, the United States was involved in the Cold War, championing the ideals of democracy against the spread of Communism. It was reluctant to criticize the South African government, which was itself such a strong opponent of Communism.

That view began to shift in the late 1950s, under pressure from the U.S. civil rights movement. Events such as the Sharpeville shootings also made it increasingly difficult to ignore the injustice of apartheid. The U.S. first expressed "regret" over apartheid and then, in 1964, banned arms sales to South Africa. Until the late 1970s, however, the U.S. government continued to see its interests linked with those of the white South African government. President Jimmy Carter, who took office in 1977, changed that emphasis. A strong supporter of human rights, he called for full political participation by all racial groups there. The United States also joined other countries in calling for an end to South African rule of Namibia (South-West Africa).

The United States still did not take firm action, however. And under President Ronald Reagan, who took office in 1981, there was less stress on human rights. The focus, again, was on U.S.-Soviet relations. The United States needed South African minerals, and it was leery of allowing the Soviets to gain influence there. For all its flaws, the South African government remained firmly opposed to Communism. Thus, while many people in the United States condemned apartheid, the government tried to steer a neutral course. Mild sanctions were imposed in 1985: banning imports of South African gold coins, restricting loans, and blocking the sale of computers to the agencies that enforce apartheid. Weak as they were, these rules were a breakthrough of sorts. But many people wanted the U.S. government to go much further.

By 1986, the value of economic sanctions and divestment was being intensely debated in the United States, in South Africa, and elsewhere, by blacks and whites alike. There were good arguments on both sides.

Those who favored sanctions argued that they represented a firm moral statement—an indication of international disapproval that the South African government would be unable to ignore. Furthermore, they said, some products obtained from abroad could be misused by the South African government; computers had been used to keep files on dissidents, and nuclear technology might be used to build weapons. (There was widespread suspicion that, with its uranium reserves, South Africa was already well on the way to becoming a nuclear power.) And beyond that, whites in South Africa both controlled industry

In the United States, students at the
University of California at Berkeley protest
the school's investment policies in companies
doing business in South Africa.

and enjoyed the greatest benefits from it. If countries around the world stopped investing in and trading with South Africa, supporters of sanctions said, white incomes would be hurt and whites would quickly pressure their governments for change.

Those who opposed sanctions argued that blacks, not whites, would be most severely hurt; they would be the ones who would lose their jobs. If the government was forced to limit spending, it would limit spending on blacks first. Moreover, most of the U.S. companies doing business in South Africa ascribe to the Sullivan Principles, a set of rules drafted by the black U.S. clergyman Leon Sullivan. These rules call for integration in work, equal pay for all races, and more nonwhites in management. European companies follow a similar code. When foreign companies left, opponents of divestment argued, their businesses were simply taken over by South African whites who did not follow the rules and often cut benefits for black workers. (Supporters of sanctions, for their part, countered that the rules weren't much help anyway because companies that adhered to them often did so in the most cursory way.)

Some people also questioned how effective trade barriers and other sanctions could be. South Africa is self-sufficient in most areas—it makes almost all the products it needs—and is said to have a ten-year supply of oil stored in abandoned gold mines. The arms embargo previously adopted only helped the country become better at making its own weapons. And the worldwide need for the minerals produced in South African mines is so great that it seems unlikely that the country would be unable to find a market for them someplace. Thus, opponents of sanctions argued, divestment and trade bans would do little to change the situation in South Africa—they would just make people in Western countries feel they were doing something about apartheid.

Both opponents and supporters of sanctions recognized that the black-ruled countries neighboring South Africa would almost certainly be hurt, however. Particularly in landlocked nations like Zimbabwe, Botswana, and Zambia, 60 to 90 percent of exports go to or through South Africa, and these countries rely on South Africa for many of their imports. Many of their workers find jobs in South African mines and industries. South Africa threatened to close its borders to trade from the north if new and broader sanctions were imposed by Europe and the United States, a move that would throw its neighbors into turmoil. Nonetheless, in 1986, Zambia and Zimbabwe announced they would adopt sanctions themselves. Other neighbors of South Africa praised their action but hung back.

South African blacks were divided on the sanctions question. Some, like Buthelezi, the leader of the Inkatha movement, opposed them as destructive. But the ANC backed sanctions strongly, as did many other black groups, as a way to force the government into action. "It is not up to the British or the Reagan Administration to tell us how much we must still suffer," Winnie Mandela said in a clandestine interview aired on British television in June 1986. "We have suffered enough." By this time many more moderate leaders, including Desmond Tutu, had come out in favor of sanctions.

In the United States the debate continued, but the movement toward sanctions gained momentum. By fall, both houses of Congress had approved measures calling for much stricter sanctions. President Reagan vetoed the plan, but its supporters had enough votes in Congress to override him. Americans were forbidden to make new investments in South African business or import products such as coal and steel from South Africa, and South African airlines were denied landing rights in the United States.

THE FUTURE

South Africa's strategic importance to the United States hasn't changed; and there is still concern that, if the ANC comes to power, Soviet influence and perhaps Communism itself will take hold. But if this would be harmful to U.S. interests, so are the cycles of violence and repression that have torn South Africa in recent years—as would be a full-scale revolution. There is also concern that, by ignoring the black resistance movements, the United States might push them toward the Soviet Union.

The best course, for South Africa and the world, is peaceful change that would bring a black majority government to power. Yet the events of recent years have made prospects for peaceful change seem dim indeed. Many observers believe that unless the South African government recognizes black demands as legitimate and deals with true black leaders, particularly the imprisoned Mandela, a bloodbath is a certainty. But the two sides remain poles apart. The government will not release Mandela unless he renounces violence, which he refuses to do unless the government itself renounces violence. Instead, it tries to negotiate with tribal leaders and others who have no real support in the black community. Nor will it entertain the idea of a black majority government, with each South African casting an equal ballot regardless of race—a point that the true black leaders insist on.

Thus the stalemate continues. And each day that it does, the chances of avoiding civil war grow slimmer. South Africa's police and military are strong. They have crushed unrest in the past, and they are probably capable of doing so again. But it would be foolish to think that they can crush it forever. A study group appointed by the Commonwealth countries in 1986 produced a grim scenario for the future: mounting political upheaval and social unrest that would disrupt the economy and spark violence throughout southern Africa. The group concluded: "A racial conflagration with frightening implications threatens."

FOR
FURTHER
READING

Increased interest about South Africa has brought a number of interesting and helpful books to U.S. stores and libraries. They range from histories and studies of apartheid, to firsthand accounts from visitors to South Africa, to works by South African writers and political figures. While the march of events ensures that many books are quickly outdated, most remain useful at least for background information.

One of the most thorough and penetrating studies of modern South Africa is *South Africa: Time Running Out*, a report prepared by the Study Commission on U.S. Policy Toward South Africa. Published in 1981 by the University of California Press and reissued in 1986 with a new introduction, the work includes a series of fascinating interviews with South Africans in all walks of life.

Other books dealing with the current situation include a wide-ranging collection of essays, *Change in Contemporary South Africa* (J. Butler and L. Thompson, eds.; University of California Press, 1975), and anthropologist Vincent Crapanzano's study of South African whites, *Waiting: The Whites of South Africa* (Random House, 1985), portions of which appeared in *The New Yorker* magazine. Roger Omond's *The Apartheid Handbook* (Viking Penguin, 1985) is a handy reference to the legal framework of apartheid. *New York Times* correspondent Joseph Lelyveld presents an unforgettable portrait of the country in *Move Your Shadow* (Times Books, 1985). Younger readers may find Clarke Newton's *Southern Africa: The Critical Land* (Dodd, Mead, 1978) helpful in understanding the region.

Useful histories include *South Africa: A Short History*, by Arthur Kepple-Jones; *South Africa: A Modern History*, by T. R. H. Davenport; and *A History of South Africa*, by Robert Lacour-Gayet. One problem shared by many older histories is a complete lack of information on early black groups—white South Africans for years enjoyed the myth that their country's history began with the arrival of Dutch colonists. In *South Africa: A Political and Economic History* (Praeger, 1966), Alex Hepple presents considerable detail on the black groups as well as later events. In *White Supremacy* (Oxford University Press, 1980), George M. Frederickson draws interesting parallels between South Africa and the United States.

Among the best known South African fiction writers who have dealt with their country's troubles are Nadine Gordimer and Doris Lessing (particularly in short stories) and Alan Paton (in *Cry, the Beloved Country* and other works). The dissident Afrikaner writer André Brink focuses on these troubles in a collection of essays, *Writing in a State of Siege* (Summit Books, 1983). Desmond Tutu has published two collections of speeches, sermons, and statements: *Crying in the Wilderness* (1982) and *Hope and Suffering* (1984). *No Easy Walk to Freedom* (Basic Books, 1965) is a collection of articles and speeches by Nelson Mandela, spanning the years 1953 to 1963. Also available in the United States are Steve Biko's *I Write What I Like* (Harper and Row, 1978) and Mangosuthu Buthelezi's *Powers Is Ours* (Books in Focus, 1979).

GLOSSARY

Afrikaans: One of the two official languages of South Africa (the other is English). It developed from seventeenth-century Dutch.

Afrikaner: A South African white descended from early Dutch, German, or Huguenot settlers.

apartheid: The South Africa policy of legalized racial segregation and discrimination. Literally, "apartness."

baas: Afrikaans word for "boss."

banning: Legal restrictions on a person's movements, associations, and speech. Can also be applied to organizations and publications.

Boer: An Afrikaner, especially a country-dweller; from Dutch word meaning "farmer."

Broederbond: A secret all-male organization founded in 1918 to further Afrikaner interests. Literally, "brotherhood."

coloured: A South African racial classification for people of mixed race, mostly African and European. Can also include Asians.

disinvestment: The selling of South African assets held by foreign companies.

divestment: The sale of stock in a corporation that has assets in South Africa.

homelands: Areas designated for the various black groups.

laager: A protective circle of wagons.

petty apartheid: Social segregation, as in transportation, sports, restaurants, and so on.

rand: Unit of South African currency.

townships: Areas near white cities designated for blacks.

trek: migration.

trekboers: White farmers who traveled on South Africa's frontiers in the 1700s and 1800s.

veld: Grassland with scattered trees.

Voortrekkers: Afrikaners who took part in the Great Trek of 1835–37.

CHRONOLOGY

900	Bantu groups established in what is now South Africa.
1488	Bartholomew Dias discovers Cape of Good Hope.
1652	First Dutch settlers arrive.
1658	First black slaves imported, from West Africa.
1659	First war with Khoikhoi.
1713	Smallpox decimates Khoikhoi.
1779	First war with Xhosa.
1795	First British occupation of the Cape.
1806	Second British occupation.
1809	Nonwhites in Cape required to carry passes and forbidden to own land.
1814	British acquire sovereignty over Cape.
1815	Slachter's Nek incident.
1828	Nonwhites given full civil rights in Cape.
1834	Cape slaves freed.
1835	Great Trek begins.
1838	Voortrekkers defeat Zulu at Blood River.
1839	Boer republic of Natalia founded.
1841	Cape Colony enacts strict master and servant laws.

1843	British annex Natal.
1844	South African Republic established in Transvaal.
1852	Sand River Convention guarantees Boer sovereignty north of the Vaal River.
1854	Boers establish Orange Free State.
1860	Indian workers begin to arrive in Natal.
1867	Diamonds discovered.
1872	Gold discovered.
1877	Britain annexes South African Republic. Ninth (last) war with Xhosa.
1880	First Boer War; South African Republic regains self-government.
1886	Major gold find on Witwatersrand.
1887	Britain annexes Zululand.
1895	Jameson Raid.
1899	Outbreak of Anglo-Boer War.
1902	End of war.
1910	Union of South Africa founded.
1911	First color bar law, for mine workers.
1912	Nationalist Party formed by Hertzog. Blacks form the South African Native National Congress, which will become African National Congress (ANC).
1914	World War I begins.
1919	In postwar settlements, South Africa gains control of South-West Africa.
1922	White workers strike and riot.
1923	Urban Areas Act restricts flow of blacks to cities.
1924	Nationalist-Labour coalition comes to power. Legislation further limits black workers' rights.
1934	National Party formed under Malan.
1936	Cape blacks removed from voters' rolls and given separate representation in Parliament.
1938	Ox Wagon Trek stirs Afrikaner nationalism.
1939	South Africa enters World War II.
1948	National Party comes to power.

1952   Nonwhite Defiance Campaign begins.

1953   Government adopts broad powers to declare state of emergency.

1954   Congress Alliance adopts Freedom Charter.

1956   Cape coloureds taken off voters' rolls and given separate representation in Parliament.

1959   Black representation in Parliament ended, to provide for "separate development" of homelands.
Separate black education system established.

1960   Sharpeville incident.
State of emergency declared; ANC and other black groups banned.

1961   South Africa becomes a republic and leaves the Commonwealth of Nations.

1963   Nelson Mandela and other black leaders arrested; mass political trials.

1964   United States joins other nations in banning arms sales to South Africa.

1976   Soweto uprising.

1977   Steve Biko dies in detention.

1979   Black labor unions legalized.

1984   New constitution gives coloureds and Indians limited power.

1985   Violence breaks out in townships; state of emergency declared in some areas.

1986   Pass laws abolished.
Sweeping state of emergency declared; press censored.
Various economic sanctions imposed by foreign nations.

INDEX

Kruger, Stephanus Paul, 51, 59
Kwazulu, 73

Laager, 44, 121
Labor, controlling, 58–62
Labour Party, 67, 86
League of Nations, 64–65
Lebowa, 74
Lembede, Anton Muziwakhe, 83
Lesotho, 23
Limpopo River, 22, 52
London Missionary Society, 39
Luthuli, Albert John, 86–87

Malan, Daniel F., 70–71
Mandela, Nelson, 83, 88, 89, 90
Mandela, Winnie, 109, 110, 116
Marriage, interracial, 71–72, 98
Mfeqane, 43
Mhlakaza, 41
Migrant workers, 106
Moshweshwe, Chief, 46, 47

Namibia, 23, 65, 113
Natal, 23, 43–45, 58–59
Natalia, 44
National Party, 83, 84, 88, 91
Nationalist Party, 64, 67, 70, 77

Native Representative Council, 68
Native (Urban Areas) Act of 1923, 65, 67
Naude, Beyers, 92, 96, 100
Ndebele, 26
New York Times, 95, 103
Newsweek, 111
Nguni, 26
Nonwhites, 58–62. *See also* Coloureds

Orange Free State, 23, 49, 54–56
Ox Wagon Trek of 1938, 69

Pan-African Congress (PAC), 87
Passbook law, 51, 75, 76, 100
Petty apartheid, 77, 97, 102, 121
Philip, John, 39
Pretorious, Andries, 44
Pretorious, Marthinus, 50
Progressive Federal Party (PFP), 96
Progressive Party, 89
Purified National Party, 69

Reagan, Ronald, 113, 116
Religion, 26, 80, 96–97
Reserves, tribal, 61, 73–75
Rhodes, Cecil John, 52, 53, 54
Riebeeck, Jan van, 29, 33
Robben Island, 28–29

Roberts, Lord, 54, 55

San, the, 24, 31–32, 34–36
Sanctions, 113-116
Sand River Convention of
  1852, 47, 50
Shaka, Chief, 43
Shantytowns, 105–106, 108
Sharpeville riots, 87
Sisulu, Albertina, 109
Sisula, Walter, 83, 85, 89
Slavery, 28, 32, 38
Smuts, Jan Christiaan, 65,
  66, 68, 70
South African Coloured
  People's Organization, 86
South African Congress of
  Democrats, 86
South African Council of
  Churches, 96
South African Indian Con-
  gress, 82, 86
South African Party, 64
South African Students'
  Organization (SASO), 93
Soviet Union, 17, 117
Soweto uprising, 93, 95–96
"State of emergency," 84, 102
Strikes, labor, 97–98
Sullivan, Leon, 115
Sullivan Principles, 115
Suzman, Helen, 89
Swart Gevaar, 64

Tambo, Oliver, 83, 101, 111
Townships, 105, 106, 121
Trade unions, 91-92

Transkei, 73, 75
Transvaal, 22, 23, 49–50, 51,
  56
Treason Trials, 86
"Treaty states," 46
Trekboers, 34, 36, 121
Tutu, Archbishop Des-
  mond, 96, 100, 109, 110,
  116

Uitlanders, 52–54
Union of South Africa, 61–
  62
Unionist Party, 65, 67
United Democratic Front,
  96, 100
United Nations, 97
United Party, 68
United States, 112–116
Urban Areas Act, 67

Vereeniging, Treaty of, 56
Verwoerd, Hendrik, 72, 87
Voortrekkers, 44–48, 121
Voting rights, 58–59, 68–69

Wages, 60, 67–68
Whites, 37–38, 78–79, 103;
  supremacy, 13, 16, 68–69
Witwatersrand, 22, 49, 52

Xhosa, 26, 36, 40–42, 73

Zambia, 116
Zimbabwe, 23, 28, 52, 116
Zulu, 26, 43–45
Zululand, 51